HUTCHINSON ENGLISH TEXTS

ANTHOLOGY OF
Modern Poetry

HUTCHINSON ENGLISH TEXTS

ANTHOLOGY OF
Modern Poetry

EDITED BY
JOHN WAIN

Hutchinson of London

Hutchinson & Co (Publishers) Ltd
3 Fitzroy Square, London W1

London Melbourne Sydney Auckland
Wellington Johannesburg and agencies
throughout the world

First published February 1963
Second impression February 1964
Third impression November 1964
Fourth impression October 1965
Fifth impression January 1968
Sixth impression April 1972
Seventh impression October 1976
Eighth impression April 1977

Printed in Great Britain by litho by The Anchor Press Ltd
and bound by Wm Brendon & Son Ltd
both of Tiptree, Essex

ISBN 0 09 067131 7 (paper non-net)

Acknowledgments

For permission to reprint copyright material the author is indebted to the following:

W. H. Auden and Faber & Faber Ltd for *Consider this and in our time, Will you turn a deaf ear* and *Chorus, Paid on both sides* from COLLECTED SHORTER POEMS; the Roy Campbell Estate for *Autumn* and *The Zulu girl* from ADAMASTOR; E. E. Cummings and Faber & Faber Ltd for *My father moved through dooms of love* from SELECTED POEMS; Lawrence Durrell and Faber & Faber Ltd for *Green Man, Nemea, To Ping-Kû, asleep* and *Dmitri of Carpathos* from COLLECTED POEMS and *Epitaph*; Miss Babette Deutsch and Indiana University Press for *Young gazelle*; Richard Eberhart and Chatto & Windus Ltd for *A young Greek, killed in the wars, The fury of aerial bombardment* and *The cancer cells* from COLLECTED POEMS; T. S. Eliot and Faber & Faber Ltd for *Gerontion*; William Empson and Chatto & Windus Ltd for *Missing dates, To an old lady* and *Manchouli* from COLLECTED POEMS; Robert Graves, Roturman S. A. and Cassell & Co. Ltd for *Mermaid, dragon, fiend, Outlaws, Ancestors, The suicide in the copse, The straw, Saint* and *Recalling war* from COLLECTED POEMS 1959; Thom Gunn and Faber & Faber Ltd for *On the move, Jesus and his mother* and *St Martin and the beggar* from SENSE OF MOVEMENT; the Trustees of the Hardy Estate and Macmillan & Co. Ltd for *Drummer Hodge, Afterwards, Transformations, To an unborn pauper child* and *The voice* from THE COLLECTED POEMS OF THOMAS HARDY; Geoffrey Hill and André Deutsch Ltd for *Requiem for the Plantagenet kings* from FOR THE UNFALLEN; Oxford University Press for *The candle indoors, The sea and the skylark, The windhover, Binsey poplars, Felix Randal* and *No worst, there is none* from THE COMPLETE BOOK OF POEMS by Gerard Manley Hopkins; Ted Hughes and Faber & Faber Ltd for *Gog* from THE NATION and *Witches* from LUPERCAL; Miss Elizabeth Jennings for *One flesh*; Routledge & Kegan Paul Ltd for *War poet* by Sidney Keyes; Miss Carolyn Kizer and Indiana University Press for *A muse of water*; Stanley Kunitz and J. M. Dent & Sons Ltd for *Benediction, The war against the trees* and *Foreign affairs* from SELECTED POEMS; Philip Larkin and The Marvell Press for *Church going* and *I remember, I remember* from THE LESS DECEIVED; Robert Lowell and Faber & Faber Ltd for *The Quaker graveyard in Nantucket* from POEMS 1938–49; Norman MacCaig and the Hogarth Press Ltd for *Laggandoan, Harris* from RIDING LIGHTS; Louis MacNeice and Faber & Faber Ltd for *Prayer before birth, The conscript, Brother fire* and *An eclogue for Christmas* from COLLECTED POEMS; John Farquharson Ltd (for the Meyerstein Estate) for *The chameleon* by E. H. W. Meyerstein; Faber & Faber Ltd for *The animals* and *The castle* from COLLECTED POEMS by Edwin Muir; Chatto & Windus Ltd for *Strange meeting* by Wilfred Owen; Miss Sylvia Plath and *The Observer* for *Morning song* and Miss Plath and William Heinemann Ltd for *Mushrooms* from THE COLOSSUS AND OTHER POEMS; Ezra Pound for *Taking leave of a friend, Canto XLV, The rest, Homage to Sextus Propertius: Section 1, Dance figure* and *Δ ὤρια*; John Crowe Ransom and Eyre & Spottiswoode Ltd for *Old man playing with children* from SELECTED POEMS; Theodore Roethke and Secker & Warburg Ltd for *The small, Snake* and *Words for the wind* from WORDS FOR THE WIND; Stephen Spender and Faber & Faber Ltd for *What I expected* and *Seascape* from COLLECTED POEMS; Faber & Faber Ltd for *Dry loaf* from COLLECTED POEMS by Wallace Stevens; Douglas Stewart, *The Bulletin* and Angus & Robertson Ltd for *The silkworms* from RUTHERFORD AND OTHER POEMS; Allen Tate and Eyre & Spottiswoode Ltd for *Ode to the confederate dead* from POEMS 1920–1945; the Trustees of the Dylan Thomas Estate and J. M. Dent & Sons Ltd for *In my craft or sullen art, The force that through the green fuse drives the flower, Poem in October, Light breaks where no sun shines, The hunchback in the park, Among those killed in the dawn raid was a man aged a hundred, A refusal to mourn the death, by fire, of a child in London* and *Do not go gentle into that good night* from COLLECTED POEMS by Dylan Thomas; R. S. Thomas and Rupert Hart-Davis Ltd for *The one furrow* from SONG AT THE YEAR'S TURNING; Terence Tiller and the Hogarth Press Ltd for *Poems for one person* from THE INWARD ANIMAL and *Street performers, 1851* from READING A MEDAL; Constantine Trypanis and Faber & Faber Ltd for *Why did I choose that man* from COCKS OF HADES and *Picture of the nativity in the church of Krena in Chios* from STONES OF TROY: Richard Wilbur and Faber & Faber Ltd for *Advice to a prophet*; William Carlos Williams and New Directions, Publishers, for *This is just to say* and *Tract* (copyright 1938, 1951) from THE COLLECTED EARLIER POEMS; and Mrs W. B. Yeats and Macmillan & Co. Ltd for *After long silence, To a friend whose work has come to nothing, Long-legged fly, Mad as the mist and snow, Lullaby, The collar-bone of a hare, An Irish airman foresees his death, A prayer for old age, Lapis lazuli, A prayer for my daughter* and *Easter 1916* from COLLECTED POEMS OF W. B. YEATS.

Acknowledgment is also due to Professor C. S. Lewis and the Syndics of Cambridge University Press for an extract from *An Experiment in Criticism*, and to Mr Peter Arnott and MacMillan & Co. Ltd for an extract from *An Introduction to the Greek Theatre*.

Contents

Preface

This book is intended to serve two purposes at once. On the one hand, it is frankly a textbook, offering (in Introduction and Notes) the essential literary-historical information about modern poetry, and (in the selection of texts) the concrete evidence of what that poetry has been, from the 1870's to the 1960's. On the other hand, it is meant to be read for pleasure. The two functions are not opposed or even clearly distinct, since any attempt to 'study' poetry without enjoying it is doomed to a particularly frustrating kind of failure.

For this reason the poets are not grouped in 'periods', but dispersed in a pattern dictated by the poems themselves. Such a method has its dangers, but its great value—if successful—is that the poems are seen in a relationship to one another, and in a common relationship to the experience of life which is their starting-point. And these things are more important than the wooden classifications of chronology. For the one fact that is clear about all the arts is that they are not sciences; they can be studied successfully only by those who remember that if you dissect life in order to examine it, what you are examining is not life.

J.W.

Introduction

I

'Modern' poetry, like modern painting and music, has now been with us for forty years. And its foundations were being laid, by certain poets in France and England, forty years before that. This puts the reader of the 1960's in an interesting position. For him the question is not 'Will modern poetry become accepted?' Rather it is 'Assuming that it has been accepted and has already enjoyed a reasonable life-span, where do we go from here?'

The fact is that the adjective 'modern', in so far as it is still used at all, tends to be taken not as a battle-cry but as a quite neutral word, simply indicating a certain period of time and a certain set of assumptions, like 'Augustan' or 'Romantic'. The term 'modern' is, admittedly, unsatisfactory and becomes more so with the passage of time; already some of the most characteristically modern poetry, making the most whole-hearted use of those techniques and attitudes which first earned the name, is beginning to seem old-fashioned. The battles have been fought, the territorial boundaries re-drawn, and many of the younger poets, finding it unnecessary to spend time and energy reliving the old days, have quietly passed on to a post-modern poetry which makes its own selections from among all the available methods.

To put it another way; if this anthology had come out in the 1920's it would, inevitably, have had to be partisan. At that time, there was still a strong, rooted body of conservative literary opinion which resisted the innovations of those poets who found themselves unable to make any real progress in the accustomed forms and therefore introduced new and unfamiliar rhythms and conventions. Ezra Pound and T. S. Eliot, by any objective standard two of the best poets of the twentieth century, were picked out for special attack, and some of the insults flung at them seem almost incredible today. (One Mr Arthur Waugh, for example, described them as 'drunken helots'. Do you get the reference? As an example of literary-critical terminology it is worth thinking over.)

Of course there was some excuse for this frightened petulance. The older generation, whose settled ways had been bombed, shelled and bayoneted to pieces in the struggle of 1914–18, were trying, understandably enough, to bend down and pick up the fragments. The temptation to pretend that the peaceful years had not come to an end, that the war had been a hideous interruption that could now be forgotten, was strong enough to cloud the judgment of many a man shrewd enough in other respects. But it was, of course, an illusion. A new epoch had come in, and if older people were not prepared to accept its ways, its manners and its art, the young were determined at least to see that they did not remain unaware of them.

Hence the 'twenties was the great age of shock and sensation. Young artists, eager to show their scorn for the stupid, narrow old ways that had led civilization into the colossal blunder of the war, took a savage delight in affronting conventional, middle-class taste. This was the epoch in which poets arranged the letters of the alphabet into arbitrary shapes and headed the result 'Poem', when music was scored for motor-horns and circular saws, when surrealist artists arranged exhibitions where the public were provided with axes with which to smash the exhibits. Even in Russia, a country where any kind of experimental art has for so many years now been out of the question, the 'twenties saw a brief flowering of modernism in its most *outré* forms; for there was, at that time, a belief in the doctrine of 'cultural Bolshevism', which maintained that violent experimentation, the sharpest possible break with conventional and academic traditions, was the fitting way of administering a 'slap in the face', as it was termed, to bourgeois Capitalist culture. (Picasso, the one great Communist painter, whose mature work has for thirty-odd years not been seen by the people of a Communist country because it runs counter to official dogma about art, is a lone survival from that brief period, like a mammoth found in a glacier.)

By 1930 the excitement about 'modern' poetry had largely spent itself; journalists still used the label in gossip-columns, and it was still common form to joke about the supposed unintelligibility of all forms of modern art; but poets themselves, intent less on news-value than on the struggle to find suitable forms in which to express their reaction to life, had quietly made their choice. Some, like Walter de la Mare, had already formed a personal style on the basis of the accustomed modes, and were able to carry on with their work without either falsifying their experience or offering a direct affront to conventional taste. Others, grouping themselves under the unquestioned leadership of Eliot, held that a new age demanded a new art; others again, like Roy Campbell, found, though they were too young to have formed their way of writing before modernism came in, that they had no need of its innovations.[1] As always, the actual living scene was far less tidy than textbook classifications would have us believe.

II

A few generalizations, however, can be applied to that first generation of modernist poets, up to about 1930. To begin with,

[1] Robert Graves, a militant champion of the new poetry, who as a critic did much to establish it, never made a sharp break with tradition in his own work; W. B. Yeats, who as an Irishman did not feel himself involved with English or American literary convention, continued to go his own way in gigantic indifference.

they were internationally minded. Like scientists, they simply could not be bothered to observe national frontiers; if a useful discovery had been made in another country they saw no reason why they should not incorporate it in their own work. Ezra Pound, a young teacher of Romance languages from Idaho, U.S.A., finding that his native country offered no current of fresh and stimulating ideas, transferred his activities to London, then to Paris and finally to Italy, keeping up a steady battle against ingrained literary insularity. T. S. Eliot, a Harvard graduate, put himself through a long and elaborate course of study at Oxford, Paris and Heidelberg. These two, of course, were Americans (a fact often resentfully quoted against them by English critics, who felt that they were interfering in the domestic affairs of English literature), though Eliot quickly took British nationality: but European poets, despite their own more tightly organized and rooted traditions, were quick to take up the same attitudes. For poets writing in English the main sources of inspiration were French; they absorbed, at first-hand or at second, the work of Baudelaire and Rimbaud, of Laforgue and Corbière. What they found in these poets was a concern with language that should render living experience in an immediate way, without throwing over it any veil of poetic mannerism; a nakedness, an honesty; a willingness to deal with the shocking and the 'unprintable'; and, not least, a savage irony which suited the disaffected post-war mood.

Secondly, they were interested in the past. Pound threw down the barriers of time as well as of geographical space, rooting for usable material in medieval French and Italian, in Latin and in Chinese; he drew particular attention to the little-known corners of European literature, such as Anglo-Saxon or Renaissance Latin. Reading his essays, and still more his letters, one has a wonderful sense of widening horizons; all good poets, in any language, have something to teach us, and 'tradition' does not mean an inert handing-on of the methods of the last hundred years. Eliot, in his famous essay *Tradition and the Individual Talent*, proposed a new and widely influential thesis: not only does the past influence the present, which of course goes without saying, but *the present influences the past*. That is to say, if a poet writes a work great enough to modify the sensibility of his readers they will then look back on the masterpieces of the past with new eyes; certain older poets can *become* important—or, conversely, fade from importance—in response to the work done by living poets; the backward look modifies the object. This explains the hostility felt towards Eliot, during those early years, by the academic fraternity, who were committed to the idea that the past is a settled landscape that can never change—that Spenser or Shelley, having once been canonized and put into examination syllabuses, are 'fixed' and can no longer be tampered with. The new criticism was impatient with Romantic poetry and much given to pointing out the virtues of poets whom the older academicism had neglected or assigned to minor positions, such as the seventeenth-century 'metaphysicals'; Eliot came out as the champion of Dryden, who in Victorian times was regarded as hardly a poet at all.

Thirdly, the modern poets had a more professional attitude to language than was then common. They wanted to pack it more densely with meaning, to make it work harder, and at the same time to relate it more closely to common speech. The rhythms and cadences of the living language, which the poet heard as he went about his daily life, were now considered the basis of all true metric. 'Poetic' language, which the reader associated with poetry and not with the way he himself talked, was to be avoided. At the same time they realized that poetry was not the same thing as ordinary conversation, otherwise there would be no need to write it. The thing to aim for was a blend of casualness and lyricism; Ezra Pound's shorter poems showed the way.

For these reasons, when the modern poets looked back over the immediate past in English poetry, they rejected most of what they found as being too 'poetic' in the wrong sense. Only a few poets were left standing: Hardy, because of his gnarled, rustic strength; Browning, here and there, because of his willingness to take risks. Gerard Manley Hopkins, whose views on poetry in many ways anticipated theirs, was at once adopted as a patron saint when his poems were published in 1918. Hopkins, a pious and diffident Jesuit priest, wrote his poems in complete isolation in the 'seventies and 'eighties; his first great masterpiece, *The Wreck of the Deutschland*, was turned down so promptly by the Catholic literary press that he never again sought publication. His work, which had so much in common with the great trail-blazing French poetry of whose existence he never knew, seemed in 1918 a confirmation of everything the modern poets believed.

III

One striking thing about the literature of the 1920's is the absence from most of it of any 'social message'. Writers like Joyce, Eliot, Forster, Aldous Huxley, did in fact have quite definite views about politics and social organization, while Ezra Pound was already moving towards those political and economic theories which were to lead to the tragic suffering of his later years; but as writers they tended to treat of larger and more general matters than the day-to-day movements of contemporary history. 'What purpose they have,' George Orwell noted, 'is very much up in the air.' In this, they were of their time, for that decade was, over most of the world, something of a breathing-space.

But the economic crash of 1929, followed by the rise of Hitler to power in Germany and the mounting threat of international Fascism, plunged the world into a different atmosphere. Germany began to rearm; Italy attacked Abyssinia; the League of Nations fell apart; England had two million unemployed; in Spain, Socialist and Fascist soldiers clashed for two and a half years in what was widely—and rightly—regarded as the first round in the coming world struggle for mastery. For ten years everybody talked politics. And the new generation of poets who began to publish soon after 1930 were naturally intent on reflecting this atmosphere in their work.

Poetry, of course, is not journalism, and there is no reason why the poet should write about the things that get into the newspaper headlines, unless he wants to. The new poets, as it happened, did want to. At any rate, W. H. Auden did, and he was so much the most brilliant and forceful of these new poets that the others accepted his leadership as naturally as poets in the 'twenties had accepted Eliot's. That is an exaggeration, but not a very big one. Auden's prestige among young poets in the 1930's was such that many of them followed him almost as if hypnotized. The political involvement of English poetry during these ten years would in any case have been considerable, for the reasons I have given; but I doubt if it would have been so great without Auden's personal influence.

This is not to say that Auden 'replaced' Eliot. It is merely that, for perfectly simple reasons, the older and more austere poet went slightly out of fashion. His politics were right-wing at a time when virtually the entire intelligentsia was socialist; his severe verbal disciplines seemed less attractive than Auden's fluency. Later, during the 1939–45 war, Eliot came into his own again with the publication of his *Four Quartets*. But the 'thirties were Auden's. Never since Pope had a poet been so widely imitated by his contemporaries. He wrote quickly and easily. Where the first generation of modern poets, with their insistence on study and discipline, their determination to re-think the basic problems of verse from a new position, had made poetry seem harder to write, Auden made it seem easier. His great gift to English poetry was to reintroduce something like the old ease of statement, without falling back on the old poetic language. He wrote as fast, and as confidently, as Byron or Browning—and yet his starting-point was not their verse, but Eliot's.

The dominance of Auden was so complete that the other poets who began at about the same time were, rather unjustly, regarded as simply henchmen and imitators. Certainly he was a strong personal example to them (a glance at Mr Spender's autobiography, *World Within World*, reveals how strong it could be), but in fact even the poets most closely associated with him never quite surrendered their own individuality. Mr MacNeice, for example, gives the impression of a poet with his mind firmly made up, one who would have written as he did even if Auden had never existed. And neither Mr Spender nor Mr Day Lewis ('MacSpaunday', Roy Campbell mockingly declared, was the composite poet of the decade) was ever entirely dominated by the young master. Still, he was the greatest single influence, and that was enough for the public.

Auden during these years was a nagger. He filled his poems with a sense of unease and menace; society, he is always saying, is in a desperate mess, and untold horrors will catch up on us unless we improve things. Above all, we must change our basic mental attitudes. Complacency, leading to blindness and a false sense of security, is the chief disease in 'this England where nobody is well'. Comfortable people, cosily enwrapped in their habits and prejudices, were not just pitiable—they were dangerous. 'Shut up talking,' he cried to them rudely,

> Shut up talking, charming in the best suits to be had in
> town,
> Lecturing on navigation while the ship is going down.

His positive recommendations varied, though the two most often indicated were Marxism and psycho-analysis. What lingers in one's mind, after reading early Auden, is not so much this or that concrete suggestion for improving the state of things as the sense of urgency that fills every line. It is too late to try to make the old ways work any longer; all must be changed; he is for 'new styles of architecture, a change of heart'.

Although, of course, the poets of the 'thirties wrote a good deal on other themes, among them the immemorial poetic themes of love, death, time, the beauty of the earth and the profounder emotions, it is this note of warning that sounds most clearly when we listen to them as a whole. In spite of the manifold troubles of that decade—unemployment, strikes, riots, the yells of dictators and the goose-stepping of storm-troopers—it was, in most Western countries, a period of super-ficial calm and plenty. A war was coming, food was being burnt and dumped in the sea to keep prices high, the unemployed were rotting in their mill-towns and mining villages: but, meanwhile, twenty cigarettes sold for less than a shilling, thirty-seven-and-six would buy a weekend in Brighton, Hobbs and Larwood were playing cricket at the Oval, Stanley Matthews was turning out for Stoke City, and George Formby was singing 'When I'm Cleaning Windows' in every big music-hall in the country. The cheaper newspapers ladled out sedative optimism (some of them were still maintaining well into 1939 that there would be no war, though anyone able to use his eyes had seen it coming unmistakeably since 1936), and popular taste in litera-ture favoured the kind of novelist (Hugh Walpole, etc.) whose work, whatever else it did, certainly made no attempt to face the actual problems of the 1930's. Against this slumbrous back-ground the younger and more alert writers sounded a con-stant Reveille. Not only the poets but the prose-writers of that generation were engaged in the task of trying to prod the snor-ing public into wakefulness—about Spain, about Hitler, about the grey-faced queues outside the Labour Exchanges. Novels like Christopher Isherwood's *Mr Norris Changes Trains* and George Orwell's *Coming Up For Air* should be read side by side with the poetry of Auden, MacNeice and Spender, to get a clear picture of the work of younger English writers during this decade. It is an impressive testimony to conscience and wakefulness in the midst of apathy and inertia.

It was natural, therefore, that the tone of most English

poetry in the 'thirties, and certainly the tone of what was still, at that time, labelled 'modern poetry', should be argumentative and public rather than introspective, private or lyrical. It was a poetry designed to recall men's minds to the reality that faced them, a reality full of danger and challenge. But, inevitably, the day came when the time for warning, for exhortation, and for the giving of reasons, was past. The grey-clad troops began to march, the swastika-painted bombers began to stream down the runways and there was no longer any point in arguing over public issues. For the next five years there was only one public issue—kill or be killed. Nobody was 'charming in the best suits to be had in town'; it was no longer necessary to raise one's voice against mass-circulation newspapers claiming that Hitler was not dangerous. And the unemployed were working at last, even if their work consisted of nothing more productive than bayonet-drill.

Poetry, as it always does, reacted to this new situation by coming up with a new idiom. Without wishing to tidy up the picture until it loses all reality, we can, I think, say that a third phase of modern poetry began in about 1940. This phase has been variously described; usually it is given some such label as 'war-time romanticism'. In any case, there is no need to argue about names. What matters is that a new idiom became general, a vast amount of verse was written in that idiom and, amid the inevitable confusion, one poet arose as the spokesman of a generation. So that to many people, looking back across twenty years, this third phase of modern poetry is simply 'the Dylan Thomas period'.

IV

The coming of the war meant that conversational, argumentative poetry suddenly lost its relevance. There was, on a political and public level, nothing much to argue about. The younger generation were taken from their homes and scattered all over the world, which meant that the sort of intellectual groups in which such arguments flourish—at universities or in capital cities—were broken up and had no chance to re-form. It was, for almost everyone, a period of loneliness, to say nothing of the ever-present uncertainty and danger. Most people who were at all actively concerned with the war, whether fighting or not, were lucky if they could say where they would be in three months' time or when they would see their friends or relatives.

In such a time poetry turns to solitary themes. In the presence of death the sense of life becomes heightened. One does not, any longer, discuss questions of what ought to be *done*. One broods, rather, on the ultimate facts, and the ultimate mysteries, of existence. And since this kind of solitary musing is more generally associated with Romantic poetry than with anything that could be called Classical, most people who feel the need to put a label to this war-time verse call it 'romanticism'. Certainly it has qualities which it shares with nineteenth-century Romantic verse: it has a high emotional temperature, it is infused with a sense of mystery, it expresses itself in language that is always reaching away from the familiar and into the unknown. And, like nineteenth-century Romanticism, when it is bad it tends to be empty, noisy, undisciplined and self-indulgent.

Inevitably, there was a great deal of bad poetry written during the war. The younger poets, impelled by the urgency of their gifts and by the drama of their situation, wrote copiously; but nearly always in isolation. There was no chance of any kind of regular contact in which the young could read and criticize one another's poems, agree on what could be successfully managed and what could not, and generally smooth the rough edges away. If very little of the verse of that time stands up today, if we find much of it impossibly over-blown, exaggerated, strained, rhetorical, all we have to do is to remember that it was produced under impossible conditions. And, remembering this, we are in a better position to appreciate, and be grateful for, the fact that the war years did, in fact, see the writing of some magnificent poetry. T. S. Eliot produced his greatest work; Robert Graves improved the already high standard of his severe yet delicate lyrics; Spender and Day Lewis both found a deeper and more authoritative note. But to most people the most compelling voice of these years, beyond a doubt, was that of Dylan Thomas.

Thomas had been publishing poetry at a fairly steady rate since 1934, when he was twenty. His work had not by any means been neglected, but during the decade of discussion it lacked the authority, or at any rate the immediately ear-catching persuasiveness, of Auden's. It was only in the changed atmosphere of 1940, when the Auden manner suddenly went dead, that Thomas was taken up, elected as a leader, and finally almost canonized, by the younger poets and the younger readers of poetry.

What 1940 needed, Thomas had. His poetry did not argue: it sang, declaimed, thundered. It did not concern itself with politics and ideas but with bedrock facts of existence: birth, death and reproduction; rocks, wind and the sea; the thrusting tendril and the eating worm. This was a poetry that made, in ringing and challenging tones, the proud claim to be entirely self-sufficient in a crumbling and dissolving world

> For all there is to give I offer:
> Crumbs, barn, and halter.

Thomas's poetry, inevitably, was condemned for being 'obscure'. And indeed its language is often so dense that paraphrase is defeated. But he is not, for all that, a difficult poet in the sense in which the Eliot of *Four Quartets* is difficult. His content is not intellectual; it is sensual and emotional.

> Especially when the October wind
> With frosty finger punishes my hair,
> Caught by the crabbing sun I walk on fire
> And cast a shadow crab upon the land,
> By the sea's side, hearing the noise of birds,
> My busy heart who shudders as she talks
> Sheds the syllabic blood and drains her words.

Those lines are from one of Thomas's early poems, written three or four years before the war; but it was, as I have said, the coming of war, with its attendant danger, loneliness and heart-break, that made Thomas's idiom seem the natural one for a whole generation. His volume *Deaths and Entrances*, published in 1946, contained the poems he had written since 1939, and, although his work is most conveniently studied in the collected edition of 1952, anyone who wants to understand the poetry of the 1940's would do well to track down a copy of *Deaths and Entrances*, in whose pages the great laments for the victims of war, such as that for 'London's daughter' or for the 'man aged a hundred', lie side by side with poems expressing joy and thanksgiving for the greenness of the earth and the presence of life in any of its forms.

I have stressed the importance of Dylan Thomas's war-time reputation, not in order to dismiss him as a mere fashion of those years but to illustrate the general point that there is always at least one poet who speaks opportunely for his hour. If Eliot was the characteristic poet of the 1920's, and Auden of the 1930's, then Thomas filled that same role in the 1940's—not because he shouldered his way into the centre of the stage but rather because the part of the stage on which he had been standing since 1934 became, suddenly, the centre. At a time when people's minds turned to the emotional and physical foundations of all experience, he wrote about those foundations. In a drab, grey, blacked-out, rationed and restricted world he splashed colour on to the page. Amid death and the possibility of death, he sang of life.

> And death shall have no dominion.
> Dead men naked they shall be one
> With the man in the wind and the west moon:
> When their bones are picked clean and the clean
>   bones gone,
> They shall have stars at elbow and foot;
> Though they go mad they shall be sane,
> Though they sink through the sea they shall
>   rise again;
> Though lovers be lost love shall not;
> And death shall have no dominion.

All these strands in Thomas's work were twisted into a stronger and finer unity by the experiences of the war years. Even his weaknesses came, in those years, to be felt as strengths. His vague religiosity, for example. Thomas himself professed no formal religion, but a good deal of the language of the Bible seeped into his poetry (he was not a Welshman for nothing), and words like 'God', 'cross', 'saint', etc., tend to make their appearance at crucial moments. This, in general, is a weakness in a poet; we feel it as such, for instance, in the poetry of D. G. Rossetti; a poet to whom religion is not a totally serious matter ought not to bring in religious trappings to decorate his verse— 'ought not', that is, not because there is a law against it but because if he does his poetry will take on a disabling air of un-reality. But in war-time there is a general feeling in the air that religious values, if not religion itself, are present; faced with, say, the consequences of an air-raid, even a complete agnostic will tend to feel that whether or not Christian beliefs are true they *ought* to be true. Even if one has no faith in the doctrines of any religion, one feels, at such moments, the sensation of having faith in what lies behind those doctrines: the ultimate mystery and the ultimate reassurance. It is this sensation that informs Thomas's poems. When he affirms, for instance, that

> After the first death, there is no other

the statement is entirely acceptable, both to a complete atheist and materialist ('since you can only live once, you can only die once') or to the most orthodox Christian who believes in eternal life. And, what is more important than mere rational assent, both atheist and Christian (and for that matter Buddhist, Confucian, Muslim, Taoist, etc., etc.) will find it a grand and consoling line. Whatever we believe or don't believe, we are nevertheless both touched and comforted by the words; after all, they are true; after the first death there *is* no other—whichever way you look at it.

The romantic manner of war-time poetry, which answered the needs of those years, ought really to have been abandoned as the 1940's wore on and the world moved into a period of uneasy peace and compromise: the period of the Iron Curtain, the Welfare State, nuclear weapons, modern jazz, NATO, the detribalization of Africa, full employment and television. The world has been different since 1945, whichever part of it you live in. And had it not been for the inevitable post-war exhaustion, the hardening of intellectual and imaginative arteries which naturally results from a long period of strain and overwork, I think there would have been a marked change in English poetry soon after 1945. As it happened, there was not. The world changed, but poetry did not. Poets went on writing in the rhetorical, highly charged manner of the earlier 'forties—which, in the uneasy calm of the later 'forties, came over simply as bombast. I do not see how any literary historian of the future will be able to avoid labelling the years 1946–50 as the nadir of twentieth-century English poetry. A blight lay on everything, a blight of pomposity and falsity. A few good poems were written, even against this background, but the poetic reputations of those years were, mostly, as two-dimensional as a film set. Mr Eliot turned from poetry to drama. Mr Auden was in America, still finding his feet in a new country, uncertain as yet of what he could, and couldn't, manage in a language that carries itself as differently as American English. Dylan Thomas, the arch-wizard, was largely silent. His energies went into broadcasts, routine film scripts and public appearances. A few long poems, saying over again in more elaborate terms what he had already said perfectly, appeared as evidence that he was marking time. This is not to say that Thomas was 'finished'; on the contrary, he was, in my opinion, on the threshold of a new and very fine period of creativity when he died in 1954. His interest was turning towards large-scale work; he wanted to write in dramatic forms, and had, at the time of his death, agreed to collaborate in an opera with Igor Stravinsky. But as a lyric poet his impetus was, at any rate for the time being, exhausted.

It was during these years that the focus of interest, in everything that concerned the poetry of the English-speaking world, moved decisively from England to America. The two literatures had remained, up to then, surprisingly wide apart, ever since American literature had developed an unmistakeable voice of its own in (roughly speaking) the 1840's. Such interchange as there was, in the years between 1900 and 1945, tended to be on the popular level; American journalism, screen plays, comic-strips and detective stories tended to influence their English equivalents, but very few serious poets or novelists, on either side of the Atlantic, knew or cared much about what was happening on the other. The giants of the first phase of modern poetry—Yeats, Eliot, Pound—were read and admired about equally in both countries, but their example did not tend to produce a uniform style in the generations that followed; American poetry during the 'thirties and 'forties is quite different from English, and on

32

the whole each tradition tended to be self-sufficient and not to borrow from the other.

During the latter part of the 'forties, however, when English poetry was becalmed in a stagnant sea, American poetry took a remarkable series of jumps forward. All at once, English poets seemed to realize that across the Atlantic was a formidable body of work which they had not studied. During the war, of course, American books were not obtainable—a situation which was prolonged until about 1948, owing to the exhaustion of Britain's purchasing power abroad and the consequent crack-down on imports. I well remember, in 1947, the excitement of a reading by Dylan Thomas in Oxford; as well as poems of his own, he read us American poems from an anthology some friend had sent him. We undergraduates were virgin soil for this winged seed. since neither we, nor any of the people concerned with our literary education, knew anything at all about modern American poetry; we were as ignorant of a poet like Wallace Stevens, who by that time had already been publishing for twenty-five years, as we were of the poets who had come to the fore during the blacked-out years. Whoever it was who had the kind thought of sending Thomas that book, he started a great many budding poets reading John Crowe Ransom, Allen Tate, Wallace Stevens, Karl Shapiro, Richard Wilbur, Robert Lowell, Marianne Moore, Randall Jarrell and a dozen more. To send a book to a poet can be as exciting and dangerous as throwing a grenade through a shop-window, and a good deal more positive.

One result of this study of American verse by younger English poets was to help them back to an understanding of, and respect for, poetic form. The American poets, however much they differed from one another in style and outlook, were united in being conscious craftsmen. American poetry has a more rhetorical tradition than English; to write poetry that demands to be read aloud, and not merely read aloud but *declaimed*, seems to come naturally to American poets. Take a poem like Allen Tate's *Ode to the Confederate Dead* and try to find anything in the work of an English poet of about the same generation (Herbert Read, say, or Edwin Muir) that has the same fine rhetorical *brio*. English poetry, when it is good, is good in a different way; more subdued, more introspective. Dylan Thomas, of course, was a rhetorical poet, coming from a country of bards; but, on the whole, the rhetoric of his poems was the quality his admirers were least able to imitate successfully.

This, I think, is one reason why, as the 'forties drifted to a close, English poets of the youngest generation began to turn towards a poetry of definite forms, of speakable rhythms, and of precise statements. They did so independently of one another, and yet by a kind of concerted impulse, like plants turning towards the sun. The shapeless, bogged-down writing that remained as a hang-over from the war years, the verse that either shambled like bad prose or, if it spoke out, did so in an embarrassingly theatrical fashion, meant less to them than the American example. But there were other reasons, of course, and deeper ones. The earliest modern poets had been formbreakers; coming into a scene where every trivial poet was an expert turner of sonnets, rondels, triolets, Spenserians, couplets, blank verse, anything the reader cared to order, they broke away into 'free' form which represented a search for spontaneity, a sharp rejection of anything that could be called 'literary', anything that suggested the study or the drawing-room rather than the places where men and women actually live their lives. This breaking of forms was essential, even though it called out the shriek of 'Drunken helots!' But thirty years had rolled by; the world had been drugged by two decades of meaningless peace and then suddenly battered nearly to death by a global war. Worse, that war had ended with the fearful savagery of Hiroshima and Nagasaki; at last man's fingers had closed round the lever that, once pulled, would bring universal destruction.

At such a time, when exhaustion and boredom in the foreground are balanced by guilt and fear in the background, it is natural that a poet should feel the impulse to *build*. Writing in regular and disciplined verse-forms is building in a simple and obvious sense, like bricklaying. Too simple, too obvious? Perhaps. But we were all very young, and we were doing the best we could to make something amid the ruins. It is easy now to smile at the 'academic' verse, as it was inevitably dubbed, that suddenly became the common idiom of the young poets of the 'fifties; easy to dismiss it as cautious, over-disciplined, lacking in the energy that makes large gestures. But we wrote like that because we had seen too much in the preceding five years of the energy that loses itself in display, the large gesture that indicates nothing. If we were cautious it was because we knew that we *had* to be better than our immediate elders, and the best way seemed to be to go to work humbly and patiently, as craftsmen, and build upwards from the ground.

I see that I have slipped into writing 'we' instead of 'they', having now brought the story up to the point where it begins to mingle with my personal memories. Which means, of course, that it is time for me to step down. I do not believe that the poetry of the 1950's and 1960's needs very much in the way of exposition and commentary; I believe that most of it deals very directly with life as we live it now, and that few poets feel the need to resort to the more violently anarchic techniques that characterized 'modern' poetry in the 'twenties. Not that those techniques are outmoded; they are available, as examples of how to bring off certain effects, just as the Elizabethan verse drama or the eighteenth-century couplet or the Romantic ode are available; once a form has been successfully realized, it passes into the bloodstream of its own particular culture, and nothing in art is ever superseded except by something better of the same kind.

Thus, if Philip Larkin's poems do not use the techniques of *The Waste Land* that is not because Larkin is seeking to overthrow and reject the achievements of the early Eliot, but merely that his own subject-matter does not require them. At the moment there seems to be a widespread impulse towards simplicity and directness; readers evidently want a poetry of this kind, and poets seem able to provide it without falling into an obviousness which would be false to the actual complexity and richness of what they want to say. The enormous public success of, say, John Betjeman, may have its dangers, for when a poet is widely popular he is usually liked for his bad qualities rather than his good ones; but the fact is that Mr Betjeman's good poems are quite as simple as his bad ones. Simplicity, when it does not go hand-in-hand with simple-mindedness, is very much in the air. To be as direct and straightforward as the poets of 1912, but without their coyness, their 'literary' artificiality, and the conventionality of their subject-matter—that seems to be the general aim of the poets of the 1960's.

Do I mean that the epoch of 'modern' poetry is over? No: merely that there are times, and this seems to be one of them, when the clash between old and new loses some of its intensity; when there is, for some years, a general willingness to see both sides of the argument. Not that it would be safe to predict the future. At any moment the revolutionary banner of some new modernity may be raised, and all the old battles break out again on a new front. For it is by such crises that poetry renews itself; and the clash of rival poetic programmes is really only the echo of a deeper struggle that is always going on—the struggle to impose the impersonal serenity of art on the hot flux of life. When anyone manages to succeed in that attempt, be he poet, musician, painter or any other kind of artist, critical comment dies on our lips, 'periods' and 'styles' are forgotten, and all we can do is to murmur, like the soothsayer in *Cymbeline*,

> The fingers of the powers above do tune
> The harmony of this peace.

Finally, I want to sound a note of warning. This anthology is intended to be useful; and it seems reasonable to suppose that the right reader—one who is prepared to read intelligently, sympathetically and *slowly*—should be able to gather, from this book alone, some idea of what 'modern' poetry has meant in the English-speaking world during the last forty-odd years: what kind of achievement it aimed at, what were its powers and also its weaknesses and dangers, and who were its main practitioners. And by carrying the selection up to very recent times —for some of these poems appeared in print only a few months before the anthology went to press—it tries hard to give a sense of the continuing struggle to write genuine poetry about the experience of living, from day to day, in our world and our society.

All this the book may possibly achieve. But there is one danger. The fact that there are no poets represented here from outside the English-speaking world may strike the thoughtless or hasty reader as an invitation to put on blinkers and indulge in an insularity that will make it impossible for him to understand modern poetry at all. For the modern idiom in poetry, as in painting, music and sculpture, is international. So much, I have indicated earlier in this Introduction; but the absence of any Continental European or Latin American representation may, for all that, give the anthology a one-sided cast. It is difficult to see how to avoid this. One day, indeed, I might indulge an old wish of mine, by making an anthology which would bring together in one book the whole contemporary Parnassus, all those modern poems which have become recognized as classics. In any case, the ideal reader of the present anthology would be aware of the *idea*, at least, of such an international collection. Behind the English and American poems in this book it is essential to be aware of the enormous shadows, and hear the pervasive echoes, of a whole world of masterpieces in other languages. My ideal anthology would contain, among much else, work by the poets Apollinaire, Valéry, Eluard, Supervielle from France, Rilke, Trakl, George and von Hoffmansthal from Germany, Montale, Quasimodo and De

Libero from Italy, Blok, Mayakovsky, Akhmatova and Pasternak from Russia, Achterberg, Vasalis, Nijhoff and de Vriess from Holland, Machado, Alberti, Jiménez and Lorca from Spain, de Andrade and Bandeira from Brazil, Paz and Huerta from Mexico, Neruda from Chile, Cavafy, Sikelianos and Seferis from Greece—the roll-call of outstanding modern poets is enormous, and many other names could be added, all acknowledged as men of genius by readers and critics in their own and other countries. The contribution of the English-speaking world has been, as it is in every age, very impressive: but I must not leave any reader, however simple or however sophisticated, with the impression that I am offering that contribution as sufficient in itself.

JOHN WAIN

Gerard Manley Hopkins
THE CANDLE INDOORS

Some candle clear burns somewhere I come by.
I muse at how its being puts blissful back
With yellowy moisture mild night's blear-all black,
Or to-fro tender trambeams truckle at the eye.
By that window what task what fingers ply,
I plod wondering, a-wanting, just for lack
Of answer the eagerer a-wanting Jessy or Jack
There God to aggrandize, God to glorify.—

Come you indoors, come home; your fading fire
Mend first and vital candle in close heart's vault:
You there are master, do your own desire;
What hinders? Are you beam-blind, yet to a fault
In a neighbour deft-handed? are you that liar
And, cast by conscience out, spendsavour salt?

Wallace Stevens
DRY LOAF

It is equal to living in a tragic land
To live in a tragic time.
Regard now the sloping, mountainous rocks

And the river that batters its way over stones,
Regard the hovels of those that live in this land.

That was what I painted behind the loaf,
The rocks not even touched by snow,
The pines along the river and the dry men blown
Brown as the bread, thinking of birds
Flying from burning countries and brown sand shores.

Birds that came like dirty water in waves
Flowing above the rocks, flowing over the sky,
As if the sky was a current that bore them along,
Spreading them as waves spread flat on the shore,
One after another washing the mountains bare.

It was the battering of drums I heard
It was hunger, it was the hungry that cried
And the waves, the waves were soldiers moving,
Marching and marching in a tragic time
Below me, on the asphalt, under the trees.

It was soldiers went marching over the rocks
And still the birds came, came in watery flocks,
Because it was spring and the birds had to come.
No doubt that soldiers had to be marching
And that drums had to be rolling, rolling, rolling.

W. H. Auden

CONSIDER THIS AND IN OUR TIME

Consider this and in our time
As the hawk sees it or the helmeted airman:
The clouds rift suddenly—look there
At cigarette-end smouldering on a border

At the first garden party of the year.
Pass on, admire the view of the massif
Through plate-glass windows of the Sport Hotel;
Join there the insufficient units
Dangerous, easy, in furs, in uniform
And constellated at reserved tables
Supplied with feelings by an efficient band
Relayed elsewhere to farmers and their dogs
Sitting in kitchens in the stormy fens.

Long ago, supreme Antagonist,
More powerful than the great northern whale
Ancient and sorry at life's limiting defect,
In Cornwall, Mendip, or the Pennine moor
Your comments on the highborn mining-captains,
Found they no answer, made them wish to die
—Lie since in barrows out of harm.
You talk to your admirers every day
By silted harbours, derelict works,
In strangled orchards, and the silent comb
Where dogs have worried or a bird was shot.
Order the ill that they attack at once:
Visit the ports and, interrupting
The leisurely conversation in the bar
Within a stone's throw of the sunlit water,
Beckon your chosen out. Summon
Those handsome and diseased youngsters, those women
Your solitary agents in the country parishes;
And mobilize the powerful forces latent
In soils that make the farmer brutal
In the infected sinus, and the eyes of stoats.
Then, ready, start your rumour, soft
But horrifying in its capacity to disgust
Which, spreading magnified, shall come to be
A polar peril, a prodigious alarm,

Scattering the people, as torn-up paper
Rags and utensils in a sudden gust,
Seized with immeasurable neurotic dread.

Financier, leaving your little room
Where the money is made but not spent,
You'll need your typist and your boy no more;
The game is up for you and for the others,
Who, thinking, pace in slippers on the lawns
Of College Quad or Cathedral Close,
Who are born nurses, who live in shorts
Sleeping with people and playing fives.
Seekers after happiness, all who follow
The convolutions of your simple wish,
It is later than you think; nearer that day
Far other than that distant afternoon
Amid rustle of frocks and stamping feet
They gave the prizes to the ruined boys.
You cannot be away, then, no
Not though you pack to leave within an hour,
Escaping humming down arterial roads:
The date was yours; the prey to fugues,
Irregular breathing and alternate ascendancies
After some haunted migratory years
To disintegrate on an instant in the explosion of mania
Or lapse for ever into a classic fatigue.

W. B. Yeats

LONG-LEGGED FLY

That civilization may not sink,
Its great battle lost,

Quiet the dog, tether the pony
To a distant post;
Our master Caesar is in the tent
Where the maps are spread,
His eyes fixed upon nothing,
A hand under his head.
Like a long-legged fly upon the stream
His mind moves upon silence.

That the topless towers be burnt
And men recall that face,
Move most gently if move you must
In this lonely place.
She thinks, part woman, three parts a child,
That nobody looks; her feet
Practise a tinker shuffle
Picked up on a street.
Like a long-legged fly upon the stream
Her mind moves upon silence.

That girls at puberty may find
The first Adam in their thought,
Shut the door of the Pope's chapel,
Keep those children out.
There on that scaffolding reclines
Michael Angelo.
With no more sound than the mice make
His hand moves to and fro.
Like a long-legged fly upon the stream
His mind moves upon silence.

Louis MacNeice

AN ECLOGUE FOR CHRISTMAS

A. I meet you in an evil time.
B.   The evil bells
   Put out of our heads, I think, the thought of everything
       else.
A. The jaded calendar revolves,
   Its nuts need oil, carbon chokes the valves,
   The excess sugar of a diabetic culture
   Rotting the nerve of life and literature;
   Therefore when we bring out the old tinsel and frills
   To announce that Christ is born among the barbarous hills
   I turn to you whom a morose routine
   Saves from the mad vertigo of being what has been.
B. Analogue of me, you are wrong to turn to me,
   My country will not yield you any sanctuary,
   There is no pinpoint in any of the ordnance maps
   To save you when your towns and town-bred thoughts
       collapse,
   It is better to die *in situ* as I shall,
   One place is as bad as another. Go back where your instincts
       call
   And listen to the crying of the town-cats and the taxis again,
   Or wind your gramophone and eavesdrop on great men.
A. Jazz-weary of years of drums and Hawaiian guitar,
   Pivoting on the parquet I seem to have moved far
   From bombs and mud and gas, have stuttered on my feet
   Clinched to the streamlined and butter-smooth trulls of the
       élite,
   The lights irritating and gyrating and rotating in gauze—
   Pomade-dazzle, a slick beauty of gewgaws—
   I who was Harlequin in the childhood of the century,
   Posed by Picasso beside an endless opaque sea,

44

Have seen myself sifted and splintered in broken facets,
Tentative pencillings, endless liabilities, no assets,
Abstractions scalpelled with a palette-knife
Without reference to this particular life.
And so it has gone on; I have not been allowed to be
Myself in flesh or face, but abstracting and dissecting me
They have made of me pure form, a symbol or a pastiche,
Stylized profile, anything but soul and flesh:
And that is why I turn this jaded music on
To forswear thought and become an automaton.

B. There are in the country also of whom I am afraid—
Men who put beer into a belly that is dead,
Women in the forties with terrier and setter who whistle and
swank
Over down and plough and Roman road and daisied
bank,
Half-conscious that these barriers over which they stride
Are nothing to the barbed wire that has grown round their
pride.

A. And two there are, as I drive in the city, who suddenly
perturb—
The one sirening me to draw up by the kerb
The other, as I lean back, my right leg stretched creating
speed,
Making me catch and stamp, the brakes shrieking, pull up
dead:
She wears silk stockings taunting the winter wind,
He carries a white stick to mark that he is blind.

B. In the country they are still hunting, in the heavy shires
Greyness is on the fields and sunset like a line of pyres
Of barbarous heroes smoulders through the ancient air
Hazed with factory dust and, orange opposite, the moon's
glare,
Goggling yokel-stubborn through the iron trees,
Jeers at the end of us, our bland ancestral ease;

We shall go down like palaeolithic man
Before some new Ice Age or Genghiz Khan.
A. It is time for some new coinage, people have got so old,
 Hacked and handled and shiny from pocketing they have
 made bold
 To think that each is himself through these accidents, being
 blind
 To the fact that they are merely the counters of an unknown
 Mind.
B. A Mind that does not think, if such a thing can be,
 Mechanical Reason, capricious Identity.
 That I could be able to face this domination nor flinch—
A. The tin toys of the hawker move on the pavement inch by
 inch
 Not knowing that they are wound up; it is better to be so
 Then to be, like us, wound up and while running down to
 know—
B. But everywhere the pretence of individuality recurs—
A. Old faces frosted with powder and choked with furs.
B. The jutlipped farmer gazing over the humpbacked wall.
A. The commercial traveller joking in the urinal.
B. I think things draw to an end, the soil is stale.
A. An over-elaboration will nothing now avail,
 The street is up again, gas, electricity or drains,
 Ever-changing conveniences, nothing comfortable remains
 Un-improved, as flagging Rome improved villa and sewer
 (A sound-proof library and a stable temperature).
 Our street is up, red lights sullenly mark
 The long trench of pipes, iron guts in the dark,
 And not till the Goths again come swarming down the hill
 Will cease the clangour of the electric drill.
 But yet there is beauty narcotic and deciduous
 In this vast organism grown out of us:
 On all the traffic-islands stand white globes like moons,
 The city's haze is clouded amber that purrs and croons,

And tilting by the noble curve bus after tall bus comes
With an osculation of yellow light, with a glory like
      chrysanthemums.

B. The country gentry cannot change, they will die in their
      shoes
From angry circumstance and moral self-abuse,
Dying with a paltry fizzle they will prove their lives to be
An ever-diluted drug, a spiritual tautology.
They cannot live once their idols are turned out,
None of them can endure, for how could they, possibly,
      without
The flotsam of private property, pekingese and polyanthus,
The good things which in the end turn to poison and
      pus,
Without the bandy chairs and the sugar in the silver tongs
And the inter-ripple and resonance of years of dinner-gongs?
Or if they could find no more that cumulative proof
In the rain dripping off the conservatory roof?
What will happen when the only sanction the country-
      dweller has—

A. What will happen to us, planked and panelled with jazz?
Who go to the theatre where a black man dances like an
      eel,
Where pink thighs flash like the spokes of a wheel, where we
      feel
That we know in advance all the jogtrot and the cake-walk
      jokes,
All the bumfun and the gags of the comedians in boaters and
      toques,
All the tricks of the virtuosos who invert the usual—

B. What will happen to us when the State takes down the
      manor wall,
When there is no more private shooting or fishing, when the
      trees are all cut down,
When faces are all dials and cannot smile or frown—

A. What will happen when the sniggering machine-guns in the
        hands of the young men
    Are trained on every flat and club and beauty parlour and
        Father's den?
    What will happen when our civilization like a long pent
        balloon—
B. What will happen will happen; the whore and the buffoon
    Will come off best; no dreamers, they cannot lose their
        dream
    And are at least likely to be reinstated in the new regime.
    But one thing is not likely—
A.   Do not gloat over yourself
    Do not be your own vulture, high on some mountain shelf
    Huddle the pitiless abstractions bald about the neck
    Who will descend when you crumple in the plains a wreck,
    Over the randy of the theatre and cinema I hear songs
    Unlike anything—
B.   The lady of the house poises the silver tongs
    And picks a lump of sugar, 'ne plus ultra' she says
    'I cannot do otherwise, even to prolong my days'—
A. I cannot do otherwise either, tonight I will book my seat—
B. I will walk about the farm-yard which is replete
    As with the smell of dung so with memories—
A. I will gorge myself to satiety with the oddities
    Of every artiste, official or amateur,
    Who has pleased me in my role of hero-worshipper
    Who has pleased me in my role of individual man—
B. Let us lie once more, say 'What we think, we can'
    The old idealist lie—
A.   And for me before I die
    Let me go the round of the garish glare—
B.   And on the bare and high
    Places of England, the Wiltshire Downs and the Long Mynd
    Let the balls of my feet bounce on the turf, my face burn in
        the wind

My eyelashes stinging in the wind, and the sheep like grey
      stones
Humble my human pretensions—
A.   Let the saxophones and the xylophones
And the cult of every technical excellence, the miles of
      canvas in the galleries
And the canvas of the rich man's yacht snapping and
      tacking on the seas
And the perfection of a grilled steak—
B.   Let all these so ephemeral things
Be somehow permanent like the swallow's tangent wings:
Goodbye to you, this day remember is Christmas, this morn
They say, interpret it your own way, Christ is born.

William Empson

MANCHOULI

I find it normal, passing these great frontiers,
That you scan the crowds in rags eagerly each side
With awe; that the nations seem real; that their ambitions
Having such achieved variety within one type, seem sane;
I find it normal;
So too to extract false comfort from that word.

Ezra Pound

TAKING LEAVE OF A FRIEND

Blue mountains to the north of the walls,
White river winding about them;
Here we must make separation
And go out through a thousand miles of dead grass.

Mind like a floating wide cloud,
Sunset like the parting of old acquaintances
Who bow over their clasped hands at a distance.
Our horses neigh to each other
     as we are departing.

                    (By Rihaku)

W. H. Auden

WILL YOU TURN A DEAF EAR

Will you turn a deaf ear
To what they said on the shore,
Interrogate their poises
In their rich houses;

Of stork-legged heaven-reachers
Of the compulsory touchers
The sensitive amusers
And masked amazers?

Yet wear no ruffian badge
Nor lie behind the hedge
Waiting with bombs of conspiracy
In arm-pit secrecy;

Carry no talisman
For germ or the abrupt pain
Needing no concrete shelter
Nor porcelain filter.

Will you wheel death anywhere
In his invalid chair,
With no affectionate instant
But his attendant?

For to be held for friend
By an undeveloped mind
To be joke for children is
Death's happiness:

Whose anecdotes betray
His favourite colour as blue
Colour of distant bells
And boys' overalls.

His tales of the bad lands
Disturb the sewing hands;
Hard to be superior
On parting nausea;

To accept the cushions from
Women against martyrdom.
Yet applauding the circuits
Of racing cyclists.

Never to make signs
Fear neither maelstrom nor zones
Salute with soldiers' wives
When the flag waves;

Remembering there is
No recognized gift for this;
No income, no bounty,
No promised country.

But to see brave sent home
Hermetically sealed with shame
And cold's victorious wrestle
With molten metal.

A neutralizing peace
And an average disgrace
Are honour to discover
For later other.

Thom Gunn

ON THE MOVE

'Man, you gotta Go'

The blue jay scuffling in the bushes follows
Some hidden purpose, and the gust of birds
That spurts across the field, the wheeling swallows,
Have nested in the trees and undergrowth
Seeking their instinct, or their poise, or both,
One moves with an uncertain violence
Under the dust thrown by a baffled sense
Or the dull thunder of approximate words.

On motorcycles, up the road, they come:
Small, black, as flies hanging in heat, the Boys,
Until the distance throws them forth, their hum
Bulges to thunder held by calf and thigh.
In goggles, donned impersonality,
In gleaming jackets trophied with the dust,
They strap in doubt—by hiding it, robust—
And almost hear a meaning in their noise.

Exact conclusion of their hardiness
Has no shape yet, but from known whereabouts
They ride, direction where the tires press.
They scare a flight of birds across the field:
Much that is natural, to the will must yield.
Men manufacture both machine and soul,

And use what they imperfectly control
To dare a future from the taken routes.

It is a part solution, after all.
One is not necessarily discord
On earth; or damned because, half animal,
One lacks direct instinct, because one wakes
Afloat on movement that divides and breaks.
One joins the movement in a valueless world,
Choosing it, till, both hurler and the hurled,
One moves as well, always toward, toward.

A minute holds them, who have come to go:
The self-defined, astride the created will
They burst away; the towns they travel through
Are home for neither bird nor holiness,
For birds and saints complete their purposes.
At worst, one is in motion; and at best,
Reaching no absolute, in which to rest,
One is always nearer by not keeping still.

California

Edwin Muir
THE CASTLE

All through that summer at ease we lay,
And daily from the turret wall
We watched the mowers in the hay
And the enemy half a mile away.
They seemed no threat to us at all.

For what, we thought, had we to fear
With our arms and provender, load on load,

Our towering battlements, tier on tier,
And friendly allies drawing near
On every leafy summer road.

Our gates were strong, our walls were thick,
So smooth and high, no man could win
A foothold there, no clever trick
Could take us, have us dead or quick.
Only a bird could have got in.

What could they offer us for bait?
Our captain was brave and we were true ...
There was a little private gate,
A little wicked wicket gate.
The wizened warder let them through.

Oh then our maze of tunnelled stone
Grew thin and treacherous as air.
The cause was lost without a groan,
The famous citadel overthrown,
And all its secret galleries bare.

How can this shameful tale be told?
I will maintain until my death
We could do nothing, being sold;
Our only enemy was gold,
And we had no arms to fight it with.

Ezra Pound

CANTO XLV

With *Usura*
With usura hath no man a house of good stone
each block cut smooth and well fitting

that design might cover their face,
with usura
hath no man a painted paradise on his church wall
harpes et luthes
or where virgin receiveth message
and halo projects from incision,
with usura
seeth no man Gonzaga his heirs and his concubines
no picture is made to endure nor to live with
but it is made to sell and sell quickly
with usura, sin against nature,
is thy bread ever more of stale rags
is thy bread dry as paper,
with no mountain wheat, no strong flour
with usura the line grows thick
with usura is no clear demarcation
and no man can find site for his dwelling.
Stone cutter is kept from his stone
weaver is kept from his loom
WITH USURA
wool comes not to market
sheep bringeth no gain with usura
Usura is a murrain, usura
blunteth the needle in the maid's hand
and stoppeth the spinner's cunning, Pietro Lombardo
came not by usura
Duccio came not by usura
nor Pier della Francesca; Zuan Bellin' not by usura
nor was 'La Calunnia' painted.
Came not by usura Angelico; came not Ambrogio Praedis,
Came no church of cut stone signed; *Adamo me fecit.*
Not by usura St Trophime
Not by usura Saint Hilaire,
Usura rusteth the chisel
It rusteth the craft and the craftsman

It gnaweth the thread in the loom
None learneth to weave gold in her pattern;
Azure hath a canker by usura; cramoisi is unbroidered
Emerald findeth no Memling
Usura slayeth the child in the womb
It stayeth the young man's courting
It hath brought palsey to bed, lyeth
between the young bride and her bridegroom
                    CONTRA NATURAM
They have brought whores for Eleusis
Corpses are set to banquet
at behest of usura.

Ezra Pound
THE REST

O helpless few in my country,
O remnant enslaved!

Artists broken against her,
A-stray, lost in the villages,
Mistrusted, spoken-against,

Lovers of beauty, starved,
Thwarted with systems,
Helpless against the control;

You who can not wear yourselves out
By persisting to successes,
You who can only speak,
Who can not steel yourselves into reiteration;

You of the finer sense,
Broken against false knowledge,

You who can know at first hand,
Hated, shut in, mistrusted:

Take thought:
I have weathered the storm,
I have beaten out my exile.

W. B. Yeats

LAPIS LAZULI

(For Harry Clifton)

I have heard that hysterical women say
They are sick of the palette and fiddle-bow,
Of poets that are always gay,
For everybody knows or else should know
That if nothing drastic is done
Aeroplane and Zeppelin will come out,
Pitch like King Billy bomb-balls in
Until the town lie beaten flat.

All perform their tragic play,
There struts Hamlet, there is Lear,
That's Ophelia, that Cordelia;
Yet they, should the last scene be there,
The great stage curtain about to drop,
If worthy their prominent part in the play,
Do not break up their lines to weep.
They know that Hamlet and Lear are gay;
Gaiety transfiguring all that dread.
All men have aimed at, found and lost;
Black out; Heaven blazing into the head:
Tragedy wrought to its uttermost.

Though Hamlet rambles and Lear rages,
And all the drop-scenes drop at once
Upon a hundred thousand stages,
It cannot grow by an inch or an ounce.

On their own feet they came, or on shipboard,
Camel-back, horse-back, ass-back, mule-back,
Old civilizations put to the sword.
Then they and their wisdom went to rack:
No handiwork of Callimachus,
Who handled marble as if it were bronze,
Made draperies that seemed to rise
When sea-wind swept the corner, stands;
His long lamp-chimney shaped like the stem
Of a slender palm, stood but a day;
All things fall and are built again,
And those that build them again are gay.

Two Chinamen, behind them a third,
Are carved in lapis lazuli,
Over them flies a long-legged bird,
A symbol of longevity;
The third, doubtless a serving-man,
Carries a musical instrument.

Every discoloration of the stone,
Every accidental crack or dent,
Seems a water-course or an avalanche,
Or lofty slope where it still snows
Though doubtless plum or cherry-branch
Sweetens the little half-way house
Those Chinamen climb towards, and I
Delight to imagine them seated there;
There, on the mountain and the sky,
On all the tragic scene they stare.

One asks for mournful melodies:
Accomplished fingers begin to play.
Their eyes mid many wrinkles, their eyes,
Their ancient, glittering eyes, are gay.

Lawrence Durrell

GREEN MAN

Four small nouns I put to pasture,
Lambs of cloud on a green paper.
My love leans like a beadle at her book,
Her smile washes the seven cities.

I am the spring's greenest publicity,
And my poem is all wrist and elbow.
O I am not daedal and need wings,
My oracle kisses a black wand.

One great verb I dip in ink
For the tortoise who carries the earth.
A grammar of fate like the map of China,
Or as wrinkles sit in the palm of a girl.

I enter my poem like a son's house.
The ancient thought is: nothing will change.
But the nouns are back in the bottle,
I ache and she is warm, was warm, is warm.

Dylan Thomas
IN MY CRAFT OR SULLEN ART

In my craft or sullen art
Exercised in the still night
When only the moon rages
And the lovers lie abed
With all their griefs in their arms,
I labour by singing light
Not for ambition or bread
Or the strut and trade of charms
On the ivory stages
But for the common wages
Of their most secret heart.

Not for the proud man apart
From the raging moon I write
On these spindrift pages
Not for the towering dead
With their nightingales and psalms
But for the lovers, their arms
Round the griefs of the ages,
Who pay no praise or wages
Nor heed my craft or art.

Ezra Pound
from HOMAGE TO SEXTUS PROPERTIUS

I

Shades of Callimachus, Coan ghosts of Philetas
It is in your grove I would walk,

I who come first from the clear font
Bringing the Grecian orgies into Italy,
                                    and the dance into Italy.
Who hath taught you so subtle a measure,
                              in what hall have you heard it;
What foot beat out your time-bar,
                        what water has mellowed your whistles?

Out-weariers of Apollo will, as we know, continue their
      Martian generalities,
            We have kept our erasers in order.
A new-fangled chariot follows the flower-hung horses;
A young Muse with young loves clustered about her
                  ascends with me into the aether, ...
And there is no high-road to the Muses.

Annalists will continue to record Roman reputations,
Celebrities from the Trans-Caucasus will belaud Roman cele-
      brities
And expound the distentions of Empire,
But for something to read in normal circumstances?
For a few pages brought down from the forked hill unsullied?'
I ask a wreath which will not crush my head.
                  And there is no hurry about it;
I shall have, doubtless, a boom after my funeral,
Seeing that long standing increases all things
                                    regardless of quality.

And who would have known the towers
                  pulled down by a deal-wood horse;
Or of Achilles withstaying waters by Simois
Or of Hector spattering wheel-rims,
Or of Polydmantus, by Scamander, or Helenus and Deiphoibos?
Their door-yards would scarcely know them, or Paris.

Small talk O Ilion, and O Troad
                                twice taken by Oetian gods,
If Homer had not stated your case!

And I also among the later nephews of this city
                                shall have my dog's day,
With no stone upon my contemptible sepulchre;
My vote coming from the temple of Phoebus in Lycia, at Patara,
And in the meantime my songs will travel,
And the devirginated young ladies will enjoy them
                                when they have got over the strangeness,
For Orpheus tamed the wild beasts—
                                and held up the Thracian river;
And Citharaon shook up the rocks by Thebes
        and danced them into a bulwark at his pleasure,
And you, O Polyphemus? Did harsh Galatea almost
Turn to your dripping horses, because of a tune, under Aetna?
We must look into the matter.
Bacchus and Apollo in favour of it,
There will be a crowd of young women doing homage to my
        palaver,
Though my house is not propped up by Taenarian columns
        from Laconia (associated with Neptune and Cerberus),
Though it is not stretched upon gilded beams;
My orchards do not lie level and wide
                                as the forests of Phaecia,
                                the luxcurious and Ionian,
Nor are my caverns stuffed stiff with a Marcian vintage,
My cellar does not date from Numa Pompilius,
Nor bristle with wine jars,
Nor is it equipped with a frigidaire patent;
Yet the companions of the Muses
                                will keep their collective nose in my books,
And weary with historical data, they will turn to my dance
        tune.

Happy who are mentioned in my pamphlets,
  the songs shall be a fine tomb-stone over their beauty.
   But against this?
Neither expensive pyramids scraping the stars in their route,
Nor houses modelled upon that of Jove in East Elis,
Nor the monumental effigies of Mausolus,
   are a complete elucidation of death.

Flame burns, rain sinks into the cracks
And they all go to rack ruin beneath the thud of the years.
Stands genius a deathless adornment,
   a name not to be worn out with the years.

Richard Eberhart
THE CANCER CELLS

Today I saw a picture of the cancer cells,
Sinister shapes with menacing attitudes,
They had outgrown their test-tube and advanced,
Sinister shapes with menacing attitudes,
Into a world beyond, a virulent laughing gang.
They looked like art itself, like the artist's mind,
Powerful shaker, and the taker of new forms.
Some are revulsed to see these spiky shapes;
It is the world of the future too come to.
Nothing could be more vivid than their language,
Lethal, sparkling and irregular stars,
The murderous design of the universe,
The hectic dance of the passionate cancer cells.
O just phenomena to the calculating eye,
Originals of imagination, I flew
With them in piled exuberance of time,

My own malignance in their racy, beautiful gestures
Quick and lean: and in their riot too
I saw the stance of the artist's make,
The fixed form in the massive fluxion.

I think Leonardo would have in his disinterest
Enjoyed them precisely with a sharp pencil.

W. B. Yeats

MAD AS THE MIST AND SNOW

Bolt and bar the shutter,
For the foul winds blow:
Our minds are at their best this night,
And I seem to know
That everything outside us is
Mad as the mist and snow.

Horace there by Homer stands,
Plato stands below,
And here is Tully's open page.
How many years ago
Were you and I unlettered lads
Mad as the mist and snow?

You ask what makes me sigh, old friend,
What makes me shudder so?
I shudder and I sigh to think
That even Cicero
And many-minded Homer were
Mad as the mist and snow.

Robert Graves

MERMAID, DRAGON, FIEND

In my childhood rumours ran
   Of a world beyond the door—
Terrors to the life of man
   That the highroad held in store.

Of the mermaids' doleful game
   In deep water I heard tell,
Or lofty dragons puffing flame,
   Or the hornèd fiend of Hell.

Tales like these were too absurd
   For my laughter-loving ear:
Soon I mocked at all I heard,
   Though with cause indeed for fear.

Now I know the mermaid kin
   I find them bound by natural laws:
They had neither tail nor fin,
   But are deadlier for that cause.

Dragons have no darting tongues,
   Teeth saw-edged nor rattling scales,
No fire issues from their lungs,
   No black poison from their tails:

For they are creatures of dark air,
   Unsubstantial tossing forms,
Thunderclaps of man's despair
   In mid-whirl of mental storms.

And there's a true and only fiend
   Worse than prophets prophesy,

Whose full powers to hurt are screened
  Lest the race of men should die.

Ever in vain will courage plot
  The dragon's death, in coat of proof;
Or love abjure the mermaid grot;
  Or faith denounce the cloven hoof.

Mermaids will not be denied
  The last bubbles of our shame,
The dragon flaunts an unpierced hide,
  The true fiend governs in God's name.

Stanley Kunitz
BENEDICTION

God banish from your house
The fly, the roach, the mouse

That riots in the walls
Until the plaster falls;

Admonish from your door
The hypocrite and liar;

No shy, soft, tigrish fear
Permit upon your stair,

Nor agents of your doubt.
God drive them whistling out.

Let nothing touched with evil,
Let nothing that can shrivel

Heart's tenderest frond, intrude
Upon your still, deep blood.

Against the drip of light
God keep all windows tight,

Protect your mirrors from
Surprise, delirium,

Admit no trailing wind
Into your shuttered mind

To plume the lake of sleep
With dreams. If you must weep

God give you tears, but leave
You secrecy to grieve,

And islands for your pride,
And love to nest in your side.

God grant that, to the bone,
Yourself may be your own;

God grant that I may be
(my sweet) sweet company.

Theodore Roethke

THE SMALL

The small birds swirl around;
The high cicadas chirr;

A towhee pecks the ground;
I look at the first star:
My heart held to its joy,
This whole September day.

The moon goes to the full;
The moon goes slowly down;
The wood becomes a wall.
Far things draw closer in.
A wind moves through the grass,
Then all is as it was.

What rustles in the fern?
I feel my flesh divide.
Things lost in sleep return
As if out of my side,
On feet that make no sound
Over the sodden ground.

The small shapes drowse: I live
To woo the fearful small;
What moves in grass I love—
The dead will not lie still,
And things throw light on things,
And all the stones have wings.

Sylvia Plath

MUSHROOMS

Overnight, very
Whitely, discreetly,
Very quietly

Our toes, our noses
Take hold on the loam,
Acquire the air.

Nobody sees us,
Stops us, betrays us;
The small grains make room.

Soft fists insist on
Heaving the needles,
The leafy bedding.

Even the paving,
Our hammers, our rams,
Earless and eyeless,

Perfectly voiceless,
Widen the crannies,
Shoulder through holes. We

Diet on water,
On crumbs of shadow,
Bland-mannered, asking

Little or nothing.
So many of us!
So many of us!

We are shelves, we are
Tables, we are meek,
We are edible,

Nudgers and shovers
In spite of ourselves.
Our kind multiplies:

We shall by morning
Inherit the earth.
Our foot's in the door.

Robert Graves

OUTLAWS

Owls—they whinny down the night;
  Bats go zigzag by.
Ambushed in shadow beyond sight
  The outlaws lie.

Old gods, tamed to silence, there
  In the wet woods they lurk,
Greedy of human stuff to snare
  In nets of murk.

Look up, else your eye will drown
  In a moving sea of black;
Between the tree-tops, upside down,
  Goes the sky-track.

Look up, else your feet will stray
  Toward that dim ambuscade
Where spider-like they trap their prey
  In webs of shade.

For though creeds whirl away in dust,
  Faith fails and men forget,
These aged gods of fright and lust
  Cling to life yet—

Old gods almost dead, malign,
　　Starved of their ancient dues—
Incense and grain, fire, blood and wine
　　And an unclean muse,

Banished to woods and a sickly moon,
　　Shrunk to mere bogey things,
Who spoke with thunder once at noon
　　To prostrate kings,

With thunder from an open sky
　　To warrior, tyrant, priest,
Bowing in fear with a dazzled eye
　　Toward the dread East—

Proud gods, humbled, sunk so low,
　　Living with ghosts and ghouls,
And ghosts of ghosts and last year's snow
　　And dead toadstools.

Edwin Muir

THE ANIMALS

They do not live in the world,
And not in time and space.
From birth to death hurled
No word do they have, not one
To plant a foot upon,
Were never in any place.

For with names the world was called
Out of the empty air,
With names was built and walled,
Line and circle and square,

Dust and emerald;
Snatched from deceiving death
By the articulate breath.

But these have never trod
Twice the familiar track,
Never never turned back
Into the memoried day.
All is new and near
In the unchanging Here
Of the fifth great day of God,
That shall remain the same,
Never shall pass away.

On the sixth day we came.

Babette Deutsch

YOUNG GAZELLE

Stiff as her Egyptian counterpart
Standing on legs of matchstick ivory,
She hides the racing of her heart,
While the black boss of her enormous eye
Flames inconsolable. Less like a deer
Than like a freckled girl, her skin's blanched gold
Drawn over little bones, her head held clear,
She listens, as if breathing were too bold.

A tremor, and she is still. Now sunny peace,
Light as the straw beneath her feet, persuades
Her pulses briefly. The terror goes—
Whipped by a childish whimsy of release,
She caracoles: a quick bound that evades
The bars. Then drops into a thrilled repose.

Gerard Manley Hopkins
THE SEA AND THE SKYLARK

On ear and ear two noises too old to end
   Trench—right, the tide that ramps against the shore;
   With a flood or a fall, low lull-off or all roar,
Frequenting there while moon shall wear and wend.

'Left hand, off land, I hear the lark ascend,
   His rash-fresh re-winded new-skeined score
   In crisps of curl off wild winch whirl, and pour
And pelt music, till none's to spill nor spend.

How these two shame this shallow and frail town!
   How ring right out our sordid turbid time,
Being pure! We, life's pride and cared-for crown,

   Have lost that cheer and charm of earth's past prime:
Our make and making break, are breaking, down
   To man's last dust, drain fast towards man's first slime.

Gerard Manley Hopkins
THE WINDHOVER

To Christ our Lord

I caught this morning morning's minion, kingdom of daylight's
   dauphin, dapple-dawn-drawn Falcon, in his riding
   Of the rolling level underneath him steady air, and striding
High there, how he rung upon the rein of a wimpling wing

In his ecstasy! then off, off forth on swing,
    As a skate's heel sweeps smooth on a bow-bend: the hurl and
      gliding
    Rebuffed the big wind. My heart in hiding
Stirred for a bird,—the achieve of, the mastery of the thing!

Brute beauty and valour and act, oh, air, pride, plume here
    Buckle! AND the fire that breaks from thee then, a billion
Times told lovelier, more dangerous, O my chevalier!

    No wonder of it: sheer plod makes plough down sillion
Shine, and blue-bleak embers, ah my dear,
    Fall, gall themselves, and gash gold-vermilion.

Theodore Roethke

SNAKE

I saw a young snake glide
Out of the mottled shade
And hang, limp on a stone:
A thin mouth, and a tongue
Stayed, in the still air.

It turned; it drew away;
Its shadow bent in half;
It quickened, and was gone.

I felt my slow blood warm.
I longed to be that thing,
The pure, sensuous form.

And I may be, some time.

Douglas Stewart
THE SILKWORMS

All their lives in a box! What generations,
What centuries of masters, not meaning to be cruel
But needing their labour, taught these creatures such patience
That now though sunlight strikes on the eye's dark jewel
Or moonlight breathes on the wing they do not stir
But like the ghosts of moths crouch silent there.

Look, it's a child's toy! There is no lid even,
They can climb, they can fly, and all the world's their tree;
But hush, they say in themselves, we are in prison.
There is no word to tell them that they are free,
And they are not; ancestral voices bind them
In dream too deep for wind or word to find them.

Even in the young, each like a little dragon
Ramping and green upon his mulberry leaf,
So full of life, it seems, the voice has spoken:
They hide where there is food, where they are safe,
And the voice whispers, 'Spin the cocoon,
Sleep, sleep, you shall be wrapped in me soon.'

Now is their hour, when they wake from that long swoon;
Their pale curved wings are marked in a pattern of leaves,
Shadowy for trees, white for the dance of the moon;
And when on summer nights the buddleia gives
Its nectar like lilac wine for insects mating
They drink its fragrance and shiver, impatient with waiting.

They stir, they think they will go. Then they remember
It was forbidden, forbidden, ever to go out;

The Hands are on guard outside like claps of thunder,
The ancestral voice says Don't, and they do not.
Still the night calls them to unimaginable bliss
But there is terror around them, the vast, the abyss,

And here is the tribe that they know, in their known place,
They are gentle and kind together, they are safe for ever,
And all shall be answered at last when they embrace.
White moth moves closer to moth, lover to lover.
There is that pang of joy on the edge of dying—
Their soft wings whirr, they dream that they are flying.

E. H. W. Meyerstein

THE CHAMELEON

His body is of lizard size,
And equalled by his tail uncurled;
His little nails are hooked; the eyes,
Wherewith he doth survey the world,
Are sunk in folds of crinkled skin
Unlatticed, never needing rest,
The while their master sleeps within
A hollow stem or grassy nest.

He feeds on air and airy things,
Which his shrewd tongue laps quickly up,
And not the thinnest pair of wings
Can flout him, when it bids him sup.
Yet, sparing ever of his food,
He lives and dies in soberness,

Moving amid the gaudy wood
Imperious in his shifting dress.

Variable chameleon,
I would that I were made as thou,
Who canst assume, by moon and sun,
The coloured world. So might I now,
Wandering in a glade of green,
Turn leaflike, or on ocean high
Take on, insensible, unseen,
A lonely wave's translucency.

Norman MacCaig

LAGGANDOAN, HARRIS

Bullock bellied in a green marsh,
Chinning his blockhead among white
And yellow tiny flowers, rolls
His brown eyes in a dark delight.

A dragon-fly of mica whirs
Off and up; then makes a thin
Tottering grass its anchor-post,
Changed to a small blue zeppelin.

And Joseph-coated frogs tumble
Like drunken heralds in the grass
That tipples sweet marsh water and
Defies the sun's broad burning-glass.

Down from the moor, between two rocks
The furnace sun has calcined white,

Johann, humped with a creel of peats,
Comes leaning forward through the light.

Then everything returns again
To timelessness. A grasshopper scours
His little pail; and blissfully
The bullock floats awash in flowers.

Gerard Manley Hopkins
BINSEY POPLARS

felled 1897

My aspens dear, whose airy cages quelled,
Quelled or quenched in leaves the leaping sun,
All felled, felled, are all felled;
    Of a fresh and following folded rank
        Not spared, not one
        That dandled a sandalled
        Shadow that swam or sank
On meadow and river and wind-wandering weed-
    winding bank.

O if we but knew what we do
        When we delve or hew—
    Hack and rack the growing green!
        Since country is so tender
    To touch, her being so slender,
    That, like this sleek and seeing ball
    But a prick will make no eye at all,
    Where we, even where we mean
        To mend her we end her,
        When we hew or delve:

After-comers cannot guess the beauty been.
Ten or twelve, only ten or twelve
Strokes of havoc unselve
The sweet especial scene,
Rural scene, a rural scene,
Sweet especial rural scene.

Stanley Kunitz

THE WAR AGAINST THE TREES

The man who sold his lawn to Standard Oil
Joked with his neighbours come to watch the show
While the bulldozers, drunk with gasoline,
Tested the virtue of the soil
Under the branchy sky
By overthrowing first the privet-row.

Forsythia-forays and hydrangea-raids
Were but preliminaries to a war
Against the great-grandfathers of the town,
So freshly lopped and maimed.
They struck and struck again,
And with each elm a century went down.

All day the hireling engines charged the trees,
Subverting them by hacking underground
In grub-dominions, where dark summer's mole
Rampages through his halls,
Till a northern seizure shook
Those crowns, forcing the giants to their knees.

I saw the ghosts of children at their games
Racing beyond their childhood in the shade,
And while the green world turned its death-foxed page
And a red wagon wheeled,
I watched them disappear
Into the suburbs of their grievous age.

Ripped from the craters much too big for hearts
The club-roots bared their amputated coils,
Raw gorgons matted blind, whose pocks and scars
Cried Moon! on a corner lot
One witness-moment, caught
In the rear-view mirrors of the passing cars.

Roy Campbell

AUTUMN

I love to see, when leaves depart,
The clear anatomy arrive,
Winter, the paragon of art,
That kills all forms of life and feeling
Save what is pure and will survive.

Already now the clanging chains
Of geese are harnessed to the moon:
Stripped are the great sun-clouding planes:
And the dark pines, their own revealing,
Let in the needles of the noon.

Strained by the gale the olives whiten
Like hoary wrestlers bent with toil

And, with the vines, their branches lighten
To brim our vats where summer lingers
In the red froth and sun-gold oil.

Soon on our hearth's reviving pyre
Their rotted stems will crumble up:
And like a ruby, panting fire,
The grape will redden on your fingers
Through the lit crystal of the cup.

Thomas Hardy

TRANSFORMATIONS

Portion of this yew
Is a man my grandsire knew,
Bosomed here at its foot:
This branch may be his wife,
A ruddy human life
Now turned to a green shoot.

These grasses must be made
Of her who often prayed,
Last century, for repose;
And the fair girl long ago
Whom I often tried to know
May be entering this rose.

So, they are not underground,
But as nerves and veins abound
In the growths of upper air,

And they feel the sun and rain,
And the energy again
That made them what they were!

Robert Graves

ANCESTORS

My New Year's drink is mulled tonight
  And hot sweet vapours roofward twine.
The shades cry *Gloria!* with delight
  As down they troop to taste old wine.

They crowd about the crackling fire,
  Impatient as the rites begin;
Mulled porto is their souls' desire—
  Porto well aged with nutmeg in.

'Ha,' cries the first, 'my Alma wine
  Of one-and-seventy years ago!'
The second cheers 'God bless the vine!'
  The third and fourth like cockerels crow:

They crow and clap their arms for wings,
  They have small pride or breeding left—
Two grey-beards, a tall youth who sings,
  A soldier with his cheek-bone cleft.

O Gloria! for each ghostly shape,
  That whiffled like a candle smoke
Now fixed and ruddy with the grape
  And mirrored at the polished oak.

I watch their brightening boastful eyes,
  I hear the toast their glasses clink:
'May this young man in drink grown wise
  Die, as we also died, in drink!'

Their reedy voices I abhor,
  I am alive at least, and young.
I dash their swill upon the floor:
  Let them lap grovelling, tongue to tongue.

W. H. Auden

CONCLUDING CHORUS FROM 'PAID ON BOTH SIDES'

Though he believe it, no man is strong.
He thinks to be called the fortunate,
To bring home a wife, to live long.

But he is defeated; let the son
Sell the farm lest the mountain fall;
His mother and her mother won.

His fields are used up where the moles visit,
The contours worn flat; if there show
Passage for water he will miss it:

Give up his breath, his woman, his team;
No life to touch, though later there be
Big fruit, eagles above the stream.

Louis MacNeice

PRAYER BEFORE BIRTH

I am not yet born; O hear me.
Let not the bloodsucking bat or the rat or the stoat or the club-
    footed ghoul come near me.

I am not yet born; console me.
I fear that the human race may with tall walls wall me,
    with strong drugs dope me, with wise lies lure me,
      on black racks rack me, in blood-baths roll me.

I am not yet born; provide me
With water to dandle me, grass to grow for me, trees to talk
    to me, sky to sing to me, birds and a white light
      in the back of my mind to guide me.

I am not yet born; forgive me
For the sins that in me the world shall commit, my words
    when they speak me, my thoughts when they think me,
      my treason engendered by traitors beyond me,
        my life when they murder by means of my
          hands, my death when they live me.

I am not yet born; rehearse me
In the parts I must play and the cues I must take when
    old men lecture me, bureaucrats hector me, mountains
      frown on me, lovers laugh at me, the white
        waves call me to folly and the desert calls
          me to doom and the beggar refuses
            my gift and my children curse me.

I am not yet born; O hear me,
Let not the man who is beast or who thinks he is God
    come near me.

I am not yet born; O fill me
With strength against those who would freeze my
    humanity, would dragoon me into a lethal automaton,
        would make me a cog in a machine, a thing with
           one face, a thing, and against all those
             who would dissipate my entirety, would
               blow me like thistledown hither and
                 thither or hither and thither
                   like water held in the
                     hands would spill me.
Let them not make me a stone and let them not spill me.
Otherwise kill me.

Thomas Hardy

TO AN UNBORN PAUPER CHILD

Breathe not, hid Heart: cease silently,
And though thy birth-hour beckons thee,
  Sleep the long sleep:
  The Doomsters heap
Travails and teens around us here,
And Time-wraiths turn our songsingings to fear.

Hark, how the people surge and sigh,
And laughters fail, and greetings die:
  Hopes dwindle; yea,
  Faiths waste away,
Affections and enthusiasms numb;
Thou canst not mend these things if thou dost come.

Had I the ear of wombed souls
Ere their terrestrial chart unrolls,
   And thou were free
   To cease, or be,
Then would I tell thee all I know,
And put it to thee: Wilt thou take Life so?

Vain vow! No hint of mine may hence
To theeward fly: to thy locked sense
   Explain none can
   Life's pending plan:
Thou wilt thy ignorant entry make
Though skies spout fire and blood and nations quake.

Fain would I, dear, find some shut plot
Of earth's wide wold for thee, where not
   One tear, one qualm,
   Should break the calm.
But I am weak as thou and bare;
No man can change the common lot to rare.

Must come and bide. And such are we—
Unreasoning, sanguine, visionary—
   That I can hope
   Health, love, friends, scope
In full for thee; can dream thou'lt find
Joys seldom yet attained by humankind!

W. B. Yeats

A PRAYER FOR MY DAUGHTER

Once more the storm is howling, and half hid
Under this cradle-hood and coverlid
My child sleeps on. There is no obstacle
But Gregory's wood and one bare hill
Whereby the haystack- and roof-levelling wind,
Bred on the Atlantic, can be stayed;
And for an hour I have walked and prayed
Because of the great gloom that is in my mind.

I have walked and prayed for this young child an hour
And heard the sea-wind scream upon the tower,
And under the arches of the bridge, and scream
In the elms above the flooded stream;
Imagining in excited reverie
That the future years had come,
Dancing to a frenzied drum,
Out of the murderous innocence of the sea.

May she be granted beauty and yet not
Beauty to make a stranger's eye distraught,
Or hers before a looking-glass, for such,
Being made beautiful overmuch,
Consider beauty a sufficient end,
Lose natural kindness and maybe
The heart-revealing intimacy
That chooses right, and never find a friend.

Helen being chosen found life flat and dull
And later had much trouble from a fool,

While that great Queen, that rose from out of the spray,
Being fatherless could have her way
Yet chose a bandy-legged smith for man.
It's certain that fine women eat
A crazy salad with their meat
Whereby the Horn of Plenty is undone.

In courtesy I'd have her chiefly learned;
Hearts are not had as a gift but hearts are earned
By those that are not entirely beautiful;
Yet many, that have played the fool
For beauty's very self, has charm made wise,
And many a poor man that has roved,
Loved and thought himself beloved,
From a glad kindness cannot take his eyes.

May she become a flourishing hidden tree
That all her thoughts may like the linnet be,
And have no business but dispensing round
Their magnanimities of sound,
Nor but in merriment begin a chase,
Nor but in merriment a quarrel.
O may she live like some green laurel
Rooted in one dear perpetual place.

My mind, because the minds that I have loved,
The sort of beauty that I have approved,
Prosper but little, has dried up of late,
Yet knows that to be choked with hate
May well be of all evil chances chief.
If there's no hatred in a mind
Assault and battery of the wind
Can never tear the linnet from the leaf.

An intellectual hatred is the worst,
So let her think opinions are accursed.

Have I not seen the loveliest woman born
Out of the mouth of Plenty's horn,
Because of her opinionated mind
Barter that horn and every good
By quiet natures understood
For an old bellows full of angry wind?

Considering that, all hatred driven hence,
The soul recovers radical innocence
And learns at last that it is self-delighting,
Self-appeasing, self-affrighting,
And that its own sweet will is Heaven's will;
She can, though every face should scowl
And every windy quarter howl
Or every bellows burst, be happy still.

And may her bridegroom bring her to a house
Where all's accustomed, ceremonious;
For arrogance and hatred are the wares
Peddled in the thoroughfares.
How but in custom and in ceremony
Are innocence and beauty born?
Ceremony's a name for the rich horn,
And custom for the spreading laurel tree.

Lawrence Durrell

TO PING-KÛ, ASLEEP

You sleeping child asleep, away
Between the confusing world of forms,
The lamplight and the day; you lie

And the pause flows through you like glass,
Asleep in the body of the nautilus.

Between comparison and sleep,
Lips that move in quotation;
The turning of a small blind mind
Like a plant everywhere ascending.
Now our love has become a beanstalk.

Invent a language where the terms
Are smiles; someone in the house now
Only understands warmth and cherish,
Still twig-bound, learning to fly.

This hand exploring the world makes
The diver's deep-sea fingers on the sills
Of underwater windows; all the wrecks
Of our world where the sad blood leads back
Through memory and sense like divers working.

Sleep, my dear, we won't disturb
You, lying in the zones of sleep.
The four walls symbolize love put about
To hold in silence which so soon brims
Over into sadness: it's still dark.

Sleep and rise a lady with a flower
Between your teeth and a cypress
Between your thighs: surely you won't ever
Be puzzled by a poem or disturbed by a poem
Made like fire by the rubbing of two sticks?

Sylvia Plath

MORNING SONG

Love set you going like a fat gold watch.
The midwife slapped your footsoles, and your bald cry
Took its place among the elements.

Our voices echo, magnifying your arrival. New statue
In a drafty museum, your nakedness
Shadows our safety. We stand round blankly as walls.

I'm no more your mother
Than the cloud that distils a mirror to reflect its own
        slow
Effacement at the wind's hand.

All night your moth-breath
Flickers among the flat pink roses. I wake to listen:
A far sea moves in my ear.

One cry, and I stumble from bed, cow-heavy and floral
In my Victorian nightgown.
Your mouth opens clean as a cat's. The window square

Whitens and swallows its dull stars. And now you try
Your handful of notes:
The clear vowels rise like balloons.

Thom Gunn

JESUS AND HIS MOTHER

My only son, more God's than mine,
Stay in this garden ripe with pears.
The yielding of their substance wears
A modest and contented shine:
And when they weep with age, not brine
But lazy syrup are their tears.
'I am my own and not my own.'

He seemed much like another man,
That silent foreigner who trod
Outside my door with lily rod:
How could I know what I began
Meeting the eyes more furious than
The eyes of Joseph, those of God?
I was my own and not my own.

And who are these twelve labouring men?
I do not understand your words:
I taught you speech, we named the birds,
You marked their big migrations then
Like any child. So turn again
To silence from the place of crowds.
'I am my own and not my own.'

Why are you sullen when I speak?
Here are your tools, the saw and knife
And hammer on your bench. Your life
Is measured here in week and week
Planed as the furniture you make,
And I will teach you like a wife
To be my own and all my own.

Who like an arrogant wind blown
Where he may please, needs no content?
Yet I remember how you went
To speak with scholars in furred gown.
I hear an outcry in the town;
Who carried that dark instrument?
'One all his own and not his own.'

Treading the green and humble sward
I stare at a strange shadow thrown.
Are you the boy I bore alone,
No doctor near to cut the cord?
I cannot reach to call you Lord,
Answer me as my only son.
'I am my own and not my own.'

Roy Campbell

THE ZULU GIRL

When in the sun the hot red acres smoulder,
Down where the sweating gang its labour plies,
A girl flings down her hoe, and from her shoulder
Unslings her child tormented by the flies.

She takes him to a ring of shadow pooled
By thorn-trees: purpled with the blood of ticks,
While her sharp nails, in slow caresses ruled,
Prowl through his hair with sharp electric clicks,

His sleepy mouth, plugged by the heavy nipple,
Tugs like a puppy, grunting as he feeds:

Through his frail nerves her own deep languors ripple
Like a broad river sighing through its reeds.

Yet in that drowsy stream his flesh imbibes
An old unquenched unsmotherable heat—
The curbed ferocity of beaten tribes,
The sullen dignity of their defeat.

Her body looms above him like a hill
Within whose shade a village lies at rest,
Or the first cloud so terrible and still
That bears the coming harvest in its breast.

Dylan Thomas

THE FORCE THAT THROUGH THE GREEN FUSE DRIVES THE FLOWER

The force that through the green fuse drives the flower
Drives my green age; that blasts the roots of trees
Is my destroyer.
And I am dumb to tell the crooked rose
My youth is bent by the same wintry fever.

The force that drives the water through the rocks
Drives my red blood; that dries the mouthing streams
Turns mine to wax.
And I am dumb to mouth unto my veins
How at the mountain spring the same mouth sucks.

The hand that whirls the water in the pool
Stirs the quicksand; that ropes the blowing wind
Hauls my shroud sail.

And I am dumb to tell the hanging man
How of my clay is made the hangman's lime.

The lips of time leech to the fountain head;
Love drips and gathers, but the fallen blood
Shall calm her sores.
And I am dumb to tell a weather's wind
How time has ticked a heaven round the stars.

And I am dumb to tell the lover's tomb
How at my sheet goes the same crooked worm.

Philip Larkin
I REMEMBER, I REMEMBER

Coming up England by a different line
For once, early in the cold new year,
We stopped, and, watching men with number-plates
Sprint down the platform to familiar gates
'Why, Coventry!' I exclaimed. 'I was born here.'

I leant far out, and squinnied for a sign
That this was still the town that had been 'mine'
So long, but found I wasn't even clear
Which side was which. From where those cycle-crates
Were standing, had we annually departed

For all those family hols? . . . A whistle went:
Things moved. I sat back, staring at my boots.
'Was that,' my friend smiled, 'where you "have your roots"?'
No, only where my childhood was unspent,
I wanted to retort, just where I started:

By now I've got the whole place clearly charted.
Our garden, first: where I did not invent
Blinding theologies of flowers and fruits,
And wasn't spoken to by an old hat.
And here we have that splendid family

I never ran to when I got depressed,
The boys all biceps and the girls all chest,
Their comic Ford, their farm where I could be
'Really myself'. I'll show you, come to that,
The bracken where I never trembling sat,

Determined to go through with it; where she
Lay back, and 'all became a burning mist'.
And, in those offices, my doggerel
Was not set up in blunt ten-point, nor read
By a distinguished cousin of the mayor,

Who didn't call and tell my father *There
Before us, had we the gift to see ahead*—
'You look as if you wished the place in Hell,'
My friend said, 'judging from your face.' 'Oh well,
I suppose it's not the place's fault,' I said.

'Nothing, like something, happens anywhere.'

Stephen Spender
WHAT I EXPECTED

What I expected was
Thunder, fighting,
Long struggles with men
And climbing.

After continual straining
I should grow strong;
Then the rocks would shake,
And I rest long.

What I had not foreseen
Was the gradual day
Weakening the will
Leaking the brightness away,
The lack of good to touch,
The fading of body and soul
—Smoke before wind,
Corrupt, unsubstantial.

The wearing of Time,
And the watching of cripples pass
With limbs shaped like questions
In their odd twist,
The pulverous grief
Melting the bones with pity,
The sick falling from earth—
These, I could not foresee.

Expecting always
Some brightness to hold in trust,
Some final innocence
Exempt from dust,
That, hanging solid,
Would dangle through all,
Like the created poem,
Or faceted crystal.

R. S. Thomas

THE ONE FURROW

When I was young, I went to school
With pencil and foot-rule
Sponge and slate,
And sat on a tall stool
At learning's gate.

When I was older, the gate swung wide;
Clever and keen-eyed
In I pressed,
But found in the mind's pride
No peace, no rest.

Then who was it taught me back to go
To cattle and barrow,
Field and plough;
To keep to the one furrow,
As I do now?

Dylan Thomas

POEM IN OCTOBER

It was my thirtieth year to heaven
Woke to my hearing from harbour and neighbour wood
And the mussel pooled and the heron
Priested shore

The morning beckon
With water praying and call of seagull and rook
And the knock of sailing boats on the net webbed wall
Myself to set foot
That second
In the still sleeping town and set forth.

My birthday began with the water—
Birds and the birds of the winged trees flying my name
Above the farms and the white horses
And I rose
In rainy autumn
And walked abroad in a shower of all my days.
High tide and the heron dived when I took the road
Over the border
And the gates
Of the town closed as the town awoke.

A springful of larks in a rolling
Cloud and the roadside bushes brimming with whistling
Blackbirds and the sun of October
Summery
On the hill's shoulder,
Here were fond climates and sweet singers suddenly
Come in the morning where I wandered and listened
To the rain wringing
Wind blow cold
In the wood faraway under me.

Pale rain over the dwindling harbour
And over the sea wet church the size of a snail
With its horns through mist and the castle
Brown as owls

But all the gardens
Of spring and summer were blooming in the tall tales
Beyond the border and under the lark full cloud.
There could I marvel
My birthday
Away but the weather turned around.

It turned away from the blithe country
And down the other air and the blue altered sky
Streamed again a wonder of summer
With apples
Pears and red currants
And I saw in the turning so clearly a child's
Forgotten mornings when he walked with his mother
Through the parables
Of sun light
And the legends of the green chapels

And the twice told fields of infancy
That his tears burned my cheeks and his heart moved in mine.
These were the woods the river and sea
Where a boy
In the listening
Summertime of the dead whispered the truth of his joy
To the trees and the stones and the fish in the tide
And the mystery
Sang alive
Still in the water and singingbirds.

And there could I marvel my birthday
Away but the weather turned around. And the true
Joy of the long dead child sang burning
In the sun.

It was my thirtieth
Year to heaven stood there then in the summer noon
Though the town below lay leaved with October blood.
O may my heart's truth
Still be sung
On this high hill in a year's turning.

Carolyn Kizer

A MUSE OF WATER

We who must act as handmaidens
To our own goddess, turn too fast,
Trip on our hems, to glimpse the muse
Gliding below her lake or sea,
Are left, long-staring after her,
Narcissists by necessity;

Or water-carriers of our young
Till waters burst, and white streams flow
Artesian, from the lifted breast:
Cup-bearers then, to tiny gods,
Imperious table-pounders, who
Are final arbiters of thirst.

Fasten the blouse, and mount the steps
From kitchen taps to Royal Barge,
Assume the trident, don the crown,
Command the Water Music now
That men bestow on Virgin Queens;
Or, goddessing above the waist,

Appear as swan on Thames or Charles
Where iridescent foam conceals
The paddle-stroke beneath the glide:
Immortal feathers preened in poems!
Not our true, intimate nature, stained
By labour, and the casual tide.

Masters of civilization, you
Who moved to river bank from cave,
Putting up tents, and deities,
Though every rivulet wander through
The final, unpolluted glades
To cinder-bank and culvert-lip,

And all the pretty chatterers
Still round the pebbles as they pass
Lightly over their watercourse,
And even the calm rivers flow,
We have, while springs and skies renew,
Dry well, dead seas, and lingering drouth.

Water itself is not enough.
Harness her turbulence to work
For man: fill his reflecting pools.
Drained for his cofferdams, or stored
In reservoirs for his personal use:
Turn switches! Let the fountains play!

And yet these buccaneers still kneel
Trembling at the water's verge:
'Cool River Goddess, sweet ravine,
Spirit of pool and shade, inspire!'
So he needs poultice for his flesh.
So he needs water for his fire.

We rose in mists and died in clouds
Or sank below the trammeled soil
To silent conduits underground,
Joining the blind-fish, and the mole,
A gleam of silver in the shale:
Lost murmur! Subterranean moan!

So flows in dark caves, dries away,
What would have brimmed from bank to bank,
Kissing the fields you turned to stone,
Under the boughs your axes broke.
And you blame streams for thinning out,
Plundered by man's insatiate want?

Rejoice when a faint music rises
Out of a brackish clump of weeds,
Out of the marsh at ocean-side,
Out of the oil-stained river's gleam,
By the long causeways and grey piers
Your civilizing lusts have made.

Discover the deserted beach
Where ghosts of curlews safely wade:
Here the warm shallows lave your feet
Like tawny hair of magdalens.
Here, if you care, and lie full-length,
Is water deep enough to drown.

Ted Hughes

WITCHES

Once was every woman the witch
To ride a weed the ragwort road;

Devil to do whatever she would:
Each rosebud, every old bitch.

Did they bargain their bodies or no?
Proprietary the devil that
Went horsing on their every thought
When they scowled the strong and lucky low.

Dancing in Ireland nightly, gone
To Norway (the ploughboy bridled),
Nightlong under the blackamoor spraddled,
Back beside their spouse by dawn

As if they had dreamed all. Did they dream it?
Oh, our science says they did.
It was all wishfully dreamed in bed.
Small psychology would unseam it.

Bitches still sulk, rosebuds blow,
And we are devilled. And though these weep
Over our harms, who's to know
Where their feet dance while their heads sleep?

Dylan Thomas

LIGHT BREAKS WHERE NO SUN SHINES

Light breaks where no sun shines;
Where no sea runs, the waters of the heart
Push in their tides;
And, broken ghosts with glow-worms in their heads,
The things of light
File through the flesh where no flesh decks the bones.

A candle in the thighs
Warms youth and seed and burns the seeds of age;
Where no seed stirs,
The fruit of man unwrinkles in the stars,
Bright as a fig;
Where no wax is, the candle shows its hairs.

Dawn breaks behind the eyes;
From poles of skull and toe the windy blood
Slides like a sea;
Nor fenced, nor staked, the gushers of the sky
Spout to the rod
Divining in a smile the oil of tears.

Night in the sockets rounds,
Like some pitch moon, the limit of the globes;
Day lights the bone;
Where no cold is, the skinning gales unpin
The winter's robes;
The film of spring is hanging from the lids.

Light breaks on secret lots,
On tips of thought where thoughts smell in the rain;
When logics die,
The secret of the soil grows through the eye,
And blood jumps in the sun;
Above the waste allotments the dawn halts.

W. B. Yeats

LULLABY

Beloved, may your sleep be sound
That have found it where you fed.

What were all the world's alarms
To mighty Paris when he found
Sleep upon a golden bed
That first dawn in Helen's arms?

Sleep, beloved, such a sleep
As did that wild Tristram know
When, the potion's work being done,
Roe could run or doe could leap
Under oak and beechen bough,
Roe could leap or doe could run;

Such a sleep and sound as fell
Upon Eurotas' grassy bank
When the holy bird, that there
Accomplished his predestined will,
From the limbs of Leda sank
But not from her protecting care.

Thomas Hardy
THE VOICE

Woman much missed, how you call to me, call to me,
Saying that now you are not as you were
When you had changed from the one who was all to me,
But as at first, when our day was fair.

Can it be you that I hear? Let me view you, then,
Standing as when I drew near to the town
Where you would wait for me: yes, as I knew you then,
Even to the original air-blue gown!

Or is it only the breeze, in its listlessness
Travelling across the wet mead to me here,
You being ever dissolved to wan wistlessness,
Heard no more again far or near?

Thus I: faltering forward,
Leaves around me falling,
Wind oozing thin through the thorn from norward,
And the woman calling.

Ezra Pound

DANCE FIGURE

For the Marriage in Cana of Galilee

Dark eyed,
O woman of my dreams,
Ivory sandaled,
There is none like thee among the dancers,
None with swift feet.

I have not found thee in the tents,
In the broken darkness
I have not found thee at the well-head
Among the women with pitchers.

Thine arms are as a young sapling under the bark;
Thy face as a river with lights.

White as an almond are thy shoulders;
As new almonds stripped from the husk.

They guard thee not with eunuchs;
Not with bars of copper.

Gilt turquoise and silver are in the place of thy rest.
A brown robe, with threads of gold woven in patterns,
      hast thou gathered about thee,
O Nathat-Ikanaie, 'Tree-at-the-river'.

As a rillet among the sedge are thy hands upon me:
Thy fingers a frosted stream.

Thy maidens are white like pebbles;
Their music about thee!

There is none like thee among the dancers;
None with swift feet.

W. B. Yeats

AFTER LONG SILENCE

Speech after long silence; it is right,
All other lovers being estranged or dead,
Unfriendly lamplight hid under its shade,
The curtains drawn upon unfriendly night,
That we descant and yet again descant
Upon the supreme theme of Art and Song:
Bodily decrepitude is wisdom: young
We loved each other and were ignorant.

Terence Tiller

POEMS FOR ONE PERSON

I

The silence that I break was more profound,
and purer, sound
—as being absent is a kind
of closer bridal, in the mind.
Nor do my words create
the peace they imitate.

Again I break with them the gentle thought
silence had brought,
painting that inward armistice
with child's, but unperspective, eyes;
in the real kiss knew yet
unions more close than it.

No threatenings then of temporal campaign
shall steal again
our spoken silence and our speech
that needs no silence each to each;
nor space nor presence mar
the better thing we are.

II

Grief is not you, nor are
the form and inward form
of you the thin despair
that whispers of your harm.
Still there are ways that leave
no valiance at all,

not of the mind but of
the inward animal:

that which is lustful in
the selves' enchanted bond,
or sees a robber when
hand is on trusting hand;
that which is death when else
I am a fire of peace,
pours tides across my pulse,
negations in my face;

the primitive revolt
against a mind or will,
the blood of Abel spilt
in cups already full.
Being and feeling and thought
are but a naked man
who fights what he is not,
the animal within:

whose fields we are; their path
the peace of me-and-you;
their long discourteous wrath
the civil war of woe.
Knowledge and now conflict;
nor have I power enough
only to live your fact
and the name of grief.

III

The lines that mathematics draw
(angular circumscription of

the curved impatience of a paw,
the eccentric swell of love)
define but cannot rule at all
the leaping inward animal.

The leaping inward animal
(the satyr in his lonely wood,
the lamb in his Wordsworthian dale)
makes every leap a maidenhead;
nor can the printed place foresee
where next those lusty feet may lie.

Where next those lusty feet may lie
(in pitfalls for the grinning wolf,
or by the writhing iron sea)
is a great sickness in itself,
whose large enfevered motions flaw
the lines that mathematics draw.

Robert Graves

THE STRAW

Peace, the wild valley streaked with torrents,
A hoopoe perched on his warm rock. Then why
This tremor of the straw between my fingers?

What should I fear? Have I not testimony
In her own hand, signed with her own name
That my love fell as lightning on her heart?

These questions, bird, are not rhetorical.
Watch how the straw twitches and leaps
As though the earth quaked at a distance.

Requited love; but better unrequited
If this chance instrument gives warning
Of cataclysmic anguish far away.

Were she at ease, warmed by the thought of me,
Would not my hand stay steady as this rock?
Have I undone her by my vehemence?

Theodore Roethke
WORDS FOR THE WIND

I

Love, love, a lily's my care,
She's sweeter than a tree.
Loving, I use the air
Most lovingly: I breathe;
Mad in the wind I wear
Myself as I should be,
All's even with the odd,
My brother the vine is glad.

Are flower and seed the same?
What do the great dead say?
Sweet Phoebe, she's my theme:
She sways whenever I sway.
'O love me while I am,
You green thing in my way!'
I cried, and the birds came down
And made my song their own.

Motion can keep me still:
She kissed me out of thought
As a lovely substance will;
She wandered; I did not:
I stayed, and light fell
Across her pulsing throat;
I stared, and a garden stone
Slowly became the moon.

The shallow stream runs slack;
The wind creaks slowly by;
Out of a nestling's beak
Comes a tremulous cry
I cannot answer back;
A shape from deep in the eye—
That woman I saw in a stone—
Keeps pace when I walk alone.

II

The sun declares the earth;
The stones leap in the stream;
On a wide plain, beyond
The far stretch of a dream,
A field breaks like the sea;
The wind's white with her name,
And I walk with the wind.

The dove's my will today.
She sways, half in the sun:
Rose, easy on a stem;
One with the sighing vine,
One to be merry with,
And pleased to meet the moon,
She likes wherever I am.

Passion's enough to give
Shape to a random joy:
I cry delight: I know
The root, the core of a cry.
Swan-heart, arbutus-calm,
She moves when time is shy:
Love has a thing to do.

A fair thing grows more fair;
The green, the springing green
Makes an intenser day
Under the rising moon;
I smile, no mineral man;
I bear, but not alone,
The burden of this joy.

III

Under a southern wind,
The birds and fishes move
North, in a single stream;
The sharp stars swing around;
I get a step beyond
The wind, and there I am,
I'm odd and full of love.

Wisdom, where is it found?—
Those who embrace, believe.
Whatever was, still is,
Says a song tied to a tree.
Below, on the ferny ground,
In rivery air, at ease,
I walk with my true love.

What time's my heart? I care.
I cherish what I have
Had of the temporal:
I am no longer young
But the winds and waters are;
What falls away will fall;
All things bring me to love.

IV

The breath of a long root,
The shy perimeter
Of the unfolding rose,
The green, the altered leaf,
The oyster's weeping foot,
And the incipient star—
Are part of what she is.
She wakes the ends of life.

Being myself, I sing
The soul's immediate joy.
Light, light, where's my repose?
A wind wreathes round a tree.
A thing is done: a thing
Body and spirit know
When I do what she does:
Creaturely creature, she!—

I kiss her moving mouth,
Her swart hilarious skin;
She breaks my breath in half;
She frolics like a beast;
And I dance round and round,
A fond and foolish man,

And see and suffer myself
In another being, at last.

W. B. Yeats

THE COLLAR-BONE OF A HARE

Would I could cast a sail on the water
Where many a king has gone
And many a king's daughter,
And alight at the comely trees and the lawn,
The playing upon pipes and the dancing,
And learn that the best thing is
To change my loves while dancing
And pay but a kiss for a kiss.

I would find by the edge of that water
The collar-bone of a hare
Worn thin by the lapping of water,
And pierce it through with a gimlet, and stare
At the old bitter world where they marry in churches,
And laugh over the untroubled water
At all who marry in churches,
Through the white thin bone of a hare.

Stanley Kunitz

FOREIGN AFFAIRS

We are two countries girded for the war,
Whisking our scouts across the pricked frontier

To ravage in each other's fields, cut lines
Along the lacework of strategic nerves,
Loot stores; while here and there,
In ambushes that trace a valley's curves,
Stark witness to the dangerous charge we bear,
A house ignites, a train's derailed, a bridge
Blows up sky-high, and water flood's the mines.
Who first attacked? Who turned the other cheek?
Aggression perpetrated is as soon
Denied, and insult rubbed into the injury
By cunning agents trained in these affairs,
With whom it's touch-and-go, don't-tread-on-me,
I-dare-you-to, keep-off, and kiss-my-hand.
Tempers could sharpen knives, and do; we live
In states provocative
Where frowning headlines scare the coffee cream
And doomsday is the eighth day of the week.

Our exit through the slammed and final door
Is twenty times rehearsed, but when we face
The imminence of cataclysmic rupture,
A lesser pride goes down upon its knees.
Two countries separated by desire!—
Whose diplomats speed back and forth by plane,
Portmanteaus stuffed with fresh apologies
Outdated by events before they land.
Negotiations wear them out: they're driven mad
Between the protocols of tears and rapture.
Locked in our fated and contiguous selves,
These worlds that too much agitate each other,
Interdependencies from hip to head,
Twin principalities both slave and free,
We coexist, proclaiming Peace together.
Tell me no lies! We are divided nations
With malcontents by thousands in our streets,

These thousands torn by inbred revolutions.
A triumph is demanded, not moral victories
Deduced from small advances, small retreats.
Are the gods of our fathers not still daemonic?
On the steps of the Capitol
The outraged lion of our years roars panic,
And we suffer the guilty cowardice of the will,
Gathering its bankrupt slogans up for flight
Like gold from ruined treasuries.
And yet, and yet, although the murmur rises,
We are what we are, and only life surprises.

William Carlos Williams
THIS IS JUST TO SAY

I have eaten
the plums
that were in
the icebox

and which
you were probably
saving
for breakfast

Forgive me
they were delicious
so sweet
and so cold

Elizabeth Jennings

ONE FLESH

Lying apart now, each in a separate bed,
He with a book, keeping the light on late,
She like a girl dreaming of childhood,
All men elsewhere—it is as if they wait
Some new event: the book he holds unread,
Her eyes fixed on the shadows overhead.

Tossed up like flotsam from a former passion,
How cool they lie. They hardly ever touch,
Or if they do it is like a confession
Of having little feeling—or too much.
Chastity faces them, a destination
For which their whole lives were a preparation.

Strangely apart and strangely close together,
Silence between them like a thread to hold
And not wind in. And time itself's a feather
Touching them gently. Do they know they're old,
These two who are my father and my mother
Whose fire, from which I came, has now grown cold?

Robert Graves

THE SUICIDE IN THE COPSE

The suicide, far from content,
Stared down at his own shattered skull:
Was this what he meant?

Had not his purpose been
To liberate himself from duns and dolts
By a change of scene?

From somewhere came a roll of laughter:
He had looked so on his wedding-day,
And the day after.

There was nowhere at all to go,
And no diversion now but to peruse
What literature the winds might blow

Into the copse where his body lay:
A year-old sheet of sporting news,
A crumpled schoolboy essay.

Dylan Thomas

THE HUNCHBACK IN THE PARK

The hunchback in the park,
A solitary mister
Propped between trees and water
From the opening of the garden lock
That lets the trees and water enter
Until the Sunday sombre bell at dark

Eating bread from a newspaper
Drinking water from the chained cup
That the children filled with gravel
In the fountain basin where I sailed my ship
Slept at night in a dog kennel
But nobody chained him up.

Like the park birds he came early
Like the water he sat down
And Mister they called Hey Mister
The truant boys from the town
Running when he had heard them clearly
On out of sound

Past lake and rockery
Laughing when he shook his paper
Hunchbacked in mockery
Through the loud zoo of the willow groves
Dodging the park keeper
With his stick that picked up leaves.

And the old dog sleeper
Alone between nurses and swans
While the boys among willows
Made the tigers jump out of their eyes
To roar on the rockery stones
And the groves were blue with sailors

Made all day until bell time
A woman figure without fault
Straight as a young elm
Straight and tall from his crooked bones
That she might stand in the night
After the locks and chains

All night in the unmade park
After the railings and shrubberies
The birds the grass the trees the lake
And the wild boys innocent as strawberries
Had followed the hunchback
To his kennel in the dark.

Lawrence Durrell

DMITRI OF CARPATHOS

Four card-players: an ikon of the saint
On a pitted table among eight hands
That cough and spit or close like mandibles
On fortunate court-cards or on the bottle
Which on the pitted paintwork stands.
Among them one whose soft transpontine nose
Fuller of dirty pores pricked on a chart
Has stood akimbo on the turning world,
From Cimbalu to Smyrna shaken hands,
Tasted the depths of every hidden sound:
In wine or poppy a drunkard with a drunkard's heart
Who never yet was known to pay his round.

Meanwhile below in harbour his rotten boat,
Beard green from winter quarters turns
Her scraggy throat to nudge the northern star,
And like a gipsy burns and burns; goes wild
Till something climbs the hill
And stands beside him at the tavern table
To pluck his drunken elbow like a child.

Thom Gunn

ST MARTIN AND THE BEGGAR

Martin sat young upon his bed
A budding cenobite,
Said 'Though I hold the principles
Of Christian life be right,

I cannot grow from them alone,
I must go out to fight.'

He travelled hard, he travelled far,
The light began to fail.
'Is not this act of mine,' he said,
'A cowardly betrayal,
Should I not peg my nature down
With a religious nail?'

Wind scudded on the marshland,
And, dangling at his side,
His sword soon clattered under hail:
What could he do but ride?—
There was not shelter for a dog,
The garrison far ahead.

A ship that moves on darkness
He rode across the plain,
When a brawny beggar started up
Who pulled at his rein
And leant dripping with sweat and water
Upon the horse's mane.

He glared into Martin's eyes
With eyes more wild than bold;
His hair sent rivers down his spine;
Like a fowl plucked to be sold
His flesh was grey. Martin said—
'What, naked in this cold?

'I have no food to give you,
Money would be a joke.'
Pulling his new sword from the sheath
He took his soldier's cloak

And cut it in two equal parts
With a single stroke.

Grabbing one to his shoulders,
Pinning it with his chin,
The beggar dived into the dark,
And soaking to the skin
Martin went on slowly
Until he reached an inn.

One candle on the wooden table,
The food and drink were poor,
The woman hobbled off, he ate,
Then casually before
The table stood the beggar as
If he had used the door.

Now dry for hair and flesh had been
By warm airs fanned,
Still bare but round each muscled thigh
A single golden band,
His eyes now wild with love, he held
The half cloak in his hand.

'You recognized the human need
Included yours, because
You did not hesitate, my saint,
To cut your cloak across;
But never since that moment
Did you regret the loss.

'My enemies would have turned away,
My holy toadies would
Have given all the cloak and frozen
Conscious that they were good.

But you, being a saint of men,
Gave only what you could.'

St Martin stretched his hand out
To offer from his plate,
But the beggar vanished, thinking food
Like cloaks is needless weight.
Pondering on the matter,
St Martin bent and ate.

Robert Graves

SAINT

This Blatant Beast was finally overcome
And in no secret tourney: wit and fashion
Flocked out and for compassion
Wept as the Red Cross Knight pushed the blade home.

The people danced and sang the paeans due,
Roasting whole oxen on the public spit;
Twelve mountain peaks were lit
With bonfires. Yet their hearts were doubt and rue.

Therefore no grave was deep enough to hold
The Beast, who after days came thrusting out,
Wormy from rump to snout,
His yellow cere-cloth patched with the grave's mould.

Nor could sea hold him: anchored with huge rocks,
He swelled and buoyed them up, paddling ashore
As evident as before
With deep-sea ooze and salty creaking bones.

Lime could not burn him, nor the sulphur-fire:
So often as the good Knight bound him there,
With stink of singeing hair
And scorching flesh the corpse rolled from the pyre.

In the city-gutter would the Beast lie
Praising the Knight for all his valorous deeds:
'Ay, on those water-meads
He slew even me. These death-wounds testify.'

The Knight governed that city, a man shamed
And shrunken: for the Beast was over-dead,
With wounds no longer red
But gangrenous and loathsome and inflamed.

Not all the righteous judgments he could utter,
Nor mild laws frame, nor public works repair,
Nor wars wage, in despair,
Could bury that same Beast, crouched in the gutter.

A fresh remembrance-banquet to forestall,
The Knight turned hermit, went without farewell
To a far mountain-cell;
But the Beast followed as his seneschal,

And there drew water for him and hewed wood
With vacant howling laughter; else all day
Noisesome with long decay
Sunning himself at the cave's entry stood.

He would bawl to pilgrims for a dole of bread
To feed the sick saint who once vanquished him
With spear so stark and grim;
Would set a pillow of grass beneath his head

Would fetch him fever-wort from the pool's brim—
And crept into his grave when he was dead.

Ted Hughes

GOG

I woke to a shout: 'I am Alpha and Omega!'
Rocks and a few trees trembled
Deep in their own country.
I ran and an absence bounded beside me.

The dog's god is a scrap dropped from the table,
The mouse's saviour is a ripe wheat grain—
Hearing the messiah cry
My mouth widens in adoration.

How far are the mosses!
They cushion themselves on the silence.
The dust, too, is replete.
The air wants for nothing.

What was my error? My skull has sealed it out.
My great bones are massed in me.
They beat on the earth, my song excites them.
I do not look at the rocks and trees, I am frightened of
        what they see.

I listen to the song jarring my mouth
Where the skull-rooted teeth are in possession.
I am massive on earth. My feetbones beat on the earth
Over the sounds of motherly weeping. . . .

Afterwards, I drink at a pool quietly,
The horizons bear the rocks and trees away into
    twilight.
I lie down, I become darkness—
Darkness that all night sings and circles stamping.

Terence Tiller

STREET PERFORMERS, 1851

Street performers . . . admit of being classified into: (a) mountebanks— or those who enact puppet-shows, as Punch and Judy, the fantoccini, and the Chinese shades . . . (b) the street-performers of feats of strength and dexterity as . . . stiff and bending tumblers, salamanders, swordsmen, etc. . . . . (c) the street performers with trained animals—as sapient pigs, dancing bears, and tame camels.

(Henry Mayhew: *London Labour and the London Poor*, 1851)

London is painted round them: burly railings
and grey rich inaccessible houses; squares—
laurelled and priveted, flowered, and fast in palings
where the grave children move and are not theirs
and are more bright and distant than the sun
whose wan dry wine shines in the windows—squares
and heavy curtains, curtains and steps of stone:
these are their coloured cards, their theatres.

Hooked nose and hump, the Black Man, the police,
the hangman's shadow by the prison wall,
the wandering misery in the courts of peace:
the mad voice like a wire will draw them all—

the puppets and the puppet-masters. Watch:
who is to tell, seeing no showmen's heads,
which are the audience, penny-foolish, which
the fantoccini and the Chinese shades?

Now (scarlet plush and gilt) the lights go on;
cold smoky curtains fold the stage away;
and all but shadows, penny plain, are gone.
Flare-cast from vehement oil, great blurs of grey
upon the gold and indigo, their dole
habit's iniquity and ungiven bread,
they drift before the rainy street; they roll
on sad wheels rags to be inherited.

The salamander and the swordsman, and
the maypole-ribboned bear: from dark they pass
to dark, through blazing islands—as if stained
in mockery upon hot slips of glass.
And the flame dies; the fingers are withdrawn;
the puppets tumble; there are no more slides;
the paints are in their boxes: they have gone,
the fantoccini and the Chinese shades.

John Crowe Ransom

OLD MAN PLAYING WITH CHILDREN

A discreet householder exclaims on the grandsire
In warpaint and feathers, with fierce grandsons and axes
Dancing round a backyard fire of boxes:
'Watch grandfather, he'll set the house on fire.'

But I will unriddle for you the thought of his mind,
An old one you cannot open with conversation.
What animates the thin legs in risky motion?
Mixes the snow on the head with snow on the wind?

'Grandson, grandsire. We are equally boy and boy.
Do not offer your reclining-chair and slippers
With tedious old women talking in wrappers.
This life is not good but in danger and in joy.

'It is you the elder to these and younger to me
Who are penned as slaves by properties and causes
And never walk from your shaped insupportable houses
And shamefully, when boys shout, go in and flee.

'May God forgive me, I know your middling ways,
Having taken care and performed ignominies unreckoned
Between the first brief childhood and the brief second,
But I will be the more honourable in these days.'

William Empson

TO AN OLD LADY

Ripeness is all; her in her cooling planet
Revere; do not presume to think her wasted.
Project her no projectile, plan nor man it;
Gods cool in turn, by the sun long outlasted.

Our earth alone given no name of god
Gives, too, no hold for such a leap to aid her;
Landing, you break some palace and seem odd;
Bees sting their need, the keeper's queen invader.

No, to your telescope; spy out the land;
Watch while her ritual is still to see,
Still stand her temples emptying in the sand
Whose waves o'erthrew their crumbling tracery;

Still stand uncalled-on her soul's appanage;
Much social detail whose successor fades,
Wit used to run a house and to play Bridge,
And tragic fervour, to dismiss her maids.

Years her procession do not throw from gear.
She reads a compass certain of her pole;
Confident, finds no confines on her sphere,
Whose failing crops are in her sole control.

Stars how much further from me fill my night.
Strange that she too should be inaccessible,
Who shares my sun. He curtains her from sight,
And but in darkness is she visible.

T. S. Eliot

GERONTION

> *Thou hast nor youth nor age*
> *But as it were an after dinner sleep*
> *Dreaming of both.*

Here I am, an old man in a dry month,
Being read to by a boy, waiting for rain.
I was neither at the hot gates
Nor fought in the warm rain

Nor knee deep in the salt marsh, heaving a cutlass,
Bitten by flies, fought.
My house is a decayed house,
And the jew squats on the window sill, the owner,
Spawned in some estaminet of Antwerp,
Blistered in Brussels, patched and peeled in London.
The goat coughs at night in the field overhead;
Rocks, moss, stonecrop, iron, merds.
The woman keeps the kitchen, makes tea,
Sneezes at evening, poking the peevish gutter.
                                        I an old man,
A dull head among windy spaces.

   Signs are taken for wonders, 'We would see a sign!'
The word within a word, unable to speak a word,
Swaddled with darkness. In the juvescence of the year
Came Christ the tiger

   In depraved May, dogwood and chestnut, flowering judas
To be eaten, to be divided, to be drunk
Among whispers; by Mr Silvero
With caressing hands, at Limoges
Who walked all night in the next room;
By Hakagwa, bowing among the Titians;
By Madame de Tornquist, in the dark room
Shifting the candles; Fräulein von Kulp
Who turned in the hall, one hand on the door. Vacant
      shuttles
Weave the wind. I have no ghosts,
An old man in a draughty house
Under a windy knob.

   After such knowledge, what forgiveness? Think now
History has many cunning passages, contrived corridors

And issues, deceives with whispering ambitions,
Guides us by vanities. Think now
She gives when our attention is distracted
And what she gives, gives with such supple confusions
That the giving famishes the craving. Gives too late
What's not believed in, or if still believed,
In memory only, reconsidered passion. Gives too soon
Into weak hands, what's thought can be dispensed with
Till the refusal propagates a fear. Think
Neither fear nor courage saves us. Unnatural vices
Are fathered by our heroism. Virtues
Are forced upon us by our impudent crimes.
These tears are shaken from the wrath-bearing tree.

The tiger springs in the new year. Us he devours.
        Think at last
We have not reached conclusion, when I
Stiffen in a rented house. Think at last
I have not made this show purposelessly
And it is not by any concitation
Of the backward devils.

I would meet you upon this honestly.
I that was near your heart was removed therefrom
To lose beauty in terror, terror in inquisition.
I have lost my passion: why would I need to keep it
Since what is kept must be adulterated?
I have lost my sight, smell, hearing, taste and touch:
How should I use them for your closer contact?

These with a thousand small deliberations
Protract the profit of their chilled delirium,
Excite the membrane, when the sense has cooled,
With pungent sauces, multiply variety

In a wilderness of mirrors. What will the spider do,
Suspend its operation, will the weevil
Delay? De Bailhache, Fresca, Mrs Cammel, whirled
Beyond the circuit of the shuddering Bear
In fractured atoms. Gull against the wind, in the windy
      straits
Of Belle Isle, or running on the Horn,
White feathers in the snow, the Gulf claims,
And an old man driven by the Trades
To a sleepy corner.

                        Tenants of the house,
Thoughts of a dry brain in a dry season.

E. E. Cummings

MY FATHER MOVED THROUGH DOOMS OF LOVE

my father moved through dooms of love
through sames of am through haves of give,
singing each morning out of each night
my father moved through depths of height

this motionless forgetful where
turned at his glance to shining here;
that if (so timid air is firm)
under his eyes would stir and squirm

newly as from unburied which
floats the first who, his april touch
drove sleeping selves to swarm their fates
woke dreamers to their ghostly roots

And should some why completely weep
my father's fingers brought her sleep:
vainly no smallest voice might cry
for he could feel the mountains grow.

Lifting the valleys of the sea
my father moved through griefs of joy;
praising a forehead called the moon
singing desire into begin

joy was his song and joy so pure
a heart of star by him could steer
and pure so now and now so yes
the wrists of twilight would rejoice

keen as midsummer's keen beyond
conceiving mind of sun will stand,
so strictly (over utmost him
so hugely) stood my father's dream

his flesh was flesh his blood was blood:
no hungry man but wished him food;
no cripple wouldn't creep one mile
uphill to only see him smile.

Scorning the pomp of must and shall
my father moved through dooms of feel;
his anger was as right as rain
his pity was as green as grain

septembering arms of year extend
less humbly wealth to foe and friend
than he to foolish and to wise
offered immeasurable is

proudly and (by octobering flame
beckoned) as earth will downward climb,
so naked for immortal work
his shoulder marched against the dark

his sorrow was as true as bread:
no liar looked him in the head;
if every friend became his foe
he'd laugh and build a world with snow.

My father moved through theys of we,
singing each new leaf out of each tree
(and every child was sure that spring
danced when she heard her father sing)

Then let men kill which cannot share,
let blood and flesh be mud and mire,
scheming imagine, passion willed,
freedom a drug that's bought and sold

giving to steal and cruel kind,
a heart to fear, to doubt a mind,
to differ a disease of same,
conform the pinnacle of am

though dull were all we taste as bright,
bitter all utterly things sweet,
maggoty minus and dumb death
all we inherit, all bequeath

and nothing quite so least as truth
—i say though hate were why men breathe
because my father lived his soul
love is the whole and more than all

Dylan Thomas

AMONG THOSE KILLED IN THE DAWN RAID WAS A MAN AGED A HUNDRED

When the morning was waking over the war
He put on his clothes and stepped out and he died,
The locks yawned loose and a blast blew them wide,
He dropped where he loved on the burst pavement stone
And the funeral grains of the slaughtered floor.
Tell his street on its back he stopped a sun
And the craters of his eyes grew springshoots and fire
When all the keys shot from the locks, and rang.
Dig no more for the chains of his grey-haired heart.
The heavenly ambulance drawn by a wound
Assembling waits for the spade's ring on the cage.
O keep his bones away from that common cart,
The morning is flying on the wings of his age
And a hundred storks perch on the sun's right hand.

Robert Graves

RECALLING WAR

Entrance and exit wounds are silvered clean,
The track aches only when the rains remind
The one-legged man forgets his leg of wood,
The one-armed man his jointed wooden arm.
The blinded man sees with his ears and hands
As much or more than once with both his eyes.
Their war was fought these twenty years ago
And now assumed the nature-look of time

As when the morning traveller turns and views
His wild night-stumbling carved into a hill.

What, then, was war? No mere discord of flags
But an infection of the common sky
That sagged ominously upon the earth
Even when the season was the airiest May.
Down pressed the sky, and we, oppressed, thrust out
Boastful tongue, clenched fist and valiant yard.
Natural infirmities were out of mode,
For Death was young again: patron alone
Of healthy dying, premature fate-spasm.

Fear made fine bed-fellows. Sick with delight
At life's discovered transitoriness,
Our youth became all-flesh and waived the mind.
Never was such antiqueness of romance,
Such tasty honey oozing from the heart.
And old importances came swimming back——
Wine, meat, log-fires, a roof over the head,
A weapon at the thigh, surgeons at call.
Even there was a use again for God—
A word of rage in lack of meat, wine, fire,
In ache of wounds beyond all surgeoning.

War was return of earth to ugly earth,
War was foundering of sublimities,
Extinction of each happy art and faith
By which the world had still kept head in air.
Protesting logic or protesting love,
Until the unendurable moment struck—
The inward scream, the duty to run mad.

And we recall the merry ways of guns—
Nibbling the walls of factory and church

Like a child, piecrust; felling groves of trees
Like a child, dandelions with a switch!
Machine-guns rattle toy-like from a hill,
Down in a row the brave tin-soldiers fall:
A sight to be recalled in elder days
When learnedly the future we devote
To yet more boastful visions of despair.

Sidney Keyes

WAR POET

I am the man who looked for peace and found
My own eyes barbed.
I am the man who groped for words and found
An arrow in my hand.
I am the builder whose firm walls surround
A slipping land.
When I grow sick or mad
Mock me not nor chain me:
When I reach for the wind
Cast me not down:
Though my face is a burnt book
And a wasted town.

Wilfred Owen

STRANGE MEETING

It seemed that out of the battle I escaped
Down some profound dull tunnel, long since scooped

Through granites which titanic wars had groined,
Yet also there encumbered sleepers groaned,
Too fast in thought or death to be bestirred.
Then, as I probed them, one sprang up, and stared
With piteous recognition in fixed eyes,
Lifting distressful hands as if to bless.
And by his smile, I knew that sullen hall;
By his dead smile I knew I stood in Hell.
With a thousand fears that vision's face was grained;
Yet no blood reached there from the upper ground,
And no guns thumped, or down the flues made moan.
'Strange friend,' I said, 'here is no cause to mourn.'
'None,' said the other, 'save the undone years,
The hopelessness. Whatever hope is yours
Was my life also; I went hunting wild
After the wildest beauty in the world,
Which lies not calm in eyes, or braided hair,
But mocks the steady running of the hour,
And if it grieves, grieves richlier than here.
For by my glee might many men have laughed,
And of my weeping something had been left
Which must die now. I mean the truth untold,
The pity of war, the pity war distilled.
Now men will go content with what we spoiled,
Or, discontent, boil bloody, and be spilled.
They will be swift with swiftness of the tigress,
None will break ranks, though nations trek from progress.
Courage was mine, and I had mystery,
Wisdom was mine, and I had mastery;
To miss the march of this retreating world
Into vain citadels that are not walled.
Then when much blood had clogged their chariot-wheels
I would go up and wash them from sweet wells,
Even with truths that lie too deep for taint.
I would have poured my spirit without stint

But not through wounds; not on the cess of war.
Foreheads of men have bled where no wounds were.
I am the enemy you killed, my friend.
I knew you in this death; for so you frowned
Yesterday through me as you jabbed and killed.
I parried; but my hands were loath and cold.
Let us sleep now. . . .'

W. B. Yeats

AN IRISH AIRMAN FORESEES HIS DEATH

I know that I shall meet my fate
Somewhere among the clouds above;
Those that I fight I do not hate,
Those that I guard I do not love;
My country is Kiltartan Cross,
My countrymen Kiltartan's poor,
No likely end could bring them loss
Or leave them happier than before.
Nor law, nor duty bade me fight,
Nor public men, nor cheering crowds,
A lonely impulse of delight
Drove to this tumult in the clouds;
I balanced all, brought all to mind,
The years to come seemed waste of breath,
A waste of breath the years behind
In balance with this life, this death.

C. A. Trypanis

WHY DID I CHOOSE THAT MAN

At some stage in our life we pick up our younger self dead off the battle-field.
W. Bethe

If we could meet our younger self, we would hardly recognize him.
K. Palamas

Why did I choose that man among the dead,
So many heaped bronze-shirted on the ground,
Blood streaking down their armour poppy-red,
Ravenous dogs and vultures circling round?

Could I have met them long before? Those eyes,
That cheek, nudging the helmet's harsh bronze cheek
Or was it through his marble sleep's disguise
Those lips, half-parted in the struggle to speak,

Muttered some secret of our earlier days —
The boy that laughing takes to the blind track,
The morning smoke unfolding through the haze
That neither words nor hands can gather back?

I heaved him into the chariot, drove away
Across the plain towards the Achaean camp.
Like trailing stars, handed from night to day,
The horses galloped down the windy ramp.

And, as I drove, I gazed down at the dead,
Jogging against the livid sky of Troy.
A broken tulip lolled his boyish head —
Myself perhaps, when half a man, half boy?

Through dust and wind how could I recognize?
And then for what? No healer now, no priest
Can coax away the sleep that drowns his eyes,
All I can give him is a burial feast.

A feast, where the Achaeans will say good-bye,
Bronze, wet with tears, and torches sadly flash,
Until on his tall pyre against the sky
The long flames lick the body into ash.

Richard Eberhart

A YOUNG GREEK,
KILLED IN THE WARS

They dug a trench, and threw him in a grave
Shallow as youth; and poured the wine out
Soaking the tunic and the dry Attic air.
They covered him lightly, and left him there.

When music comes upon the airs of Spring,
Faith fevers the blood; counter to harmony,
The mind makes its rugged testaments.
Melancholy moves, preservative and predatory.

The light is a container of treachery,
The light is the preserver of the Parthenon.
The light is lost from that young eye.
Hearing music, I speak, lest he should die.

Louis MacNeice

THE CONSCRIPT

Being so young he feels the weight of history
Like clay around his boots; he would, if he could, fly
In search of a future like a sycamore seed
But is prevented by his own Necessity
His own yet alien, which, whatever he may plead,
To every question gives the same reply.

Choiceless therefore, driven from pillar to post,
Expiating his pedigree, fulfilling
An oracle whose returns grow less and less,
Bandied from camp to camp to practise killing
He fails even so at times to remain engrossed
And is aware, at times, of life's largesse.

From camp to camp, from Eocene to chalk,
He lives a paradox, lives in a groove
That runs dead straight to an ordained disaster
So that in two dimensions he must move
Like an automaton, yet his inward stalk
Vertically aspires and makes him his own master.

Hence, though on the flat his life has no
Promise but of diminishing returns,
By feeling down and upwards he can divine
That dignity which far above him burns
In stars that yet are his and which below
Stands rooted like a dolmen in his spine.

W. B. Yeats

EASTER 1916

I have met them at close of day
Coming with vivid faces
From counter or desk among grey
Eighteenth-century houses.
I have passed with a nod of the head
Or polite meaningless words,
Or have lingered awhile and said
Polite meaningless words,
And thought before I had done
Of a mocking tale or a gibe
To please a companion
Around the fire at the club,
Being certain that they and I
But lived where motley is worn:
All changed, changed utterly:
A terrible beauty is born.

That woman's days were spent
In ignorant goodwill,
Her nights in argument
Until her voice grew shrill.
What voice more sweet than hers
When, young and beautiful,
She rode to harriers?
This man had kept a school
And rode our winged horse;
This other his helper and friend
Was coming into his force;
He might have won fame in the end,
So sensitive his nature seemed,

So daring and sweet his thought.
This other man I had dreamed
A drunken, vainglorious lout.
He had done most bitter wrong
To some who are near my heart,
Yet I number him in the song;
He, too, has resigned his part
In the casual comedy;
He, too, has been changed in his turn,
Transformed utterly:
A terrible beauty is born.

Hearts with one purpose alone
Through summer and winter seem
Enchanted to a stone
To trouble the living stream.
The horse that comes from the road,
The rider, the birds that range
From cloud to tumbling cloud,
Minute by minute they change;
A shadow of cloud on the stream
Changes minute by minute;
A horsehoof slides on the brim,
And a horse plashes within it;
The long-legged moor-hens dive,
And hens to moor-cocks call;
Minute by minute they live:
The stone's in the midst of all.

Too long a sacrifice
Can make a stone of the heart.
O when may it suffice?
That is Heaven's part, our part
To murmur name upon name,
As a mother names her child

When sleep at last has come
On limbs that had run wild.
What is it but nightfall?
No, no, not night but death;
Was it needless death after all?
For England may keep faith
For all that is done and said.
We know their dream; enough
To know they dreamed and are dead;
And what if excess of love
Bewildered them till they died?
I write it out in a verse—
MacDonagh and MacBride
And Connolly and Pearse
Now and in time to be,
Wherever green is worn,
Are changed, changed utterly:
A terrible beauty is born.

25 September 1916

Allen Tate

ODE TO THE CONFEDERATE DEAD

Row after row with strict impunity
The headstones yield their names to the element,
The wind whirrs without recollection;
In the riven troughs the splayed leaves
Pile up, of nature the casual sacrament
To the seasonal eternity of death;
Then driven by the fierce scrutiny

Of heaven to the election in the vast breath,
They sough the rumour of mortality.

Autumn is desolation in the plot
Of a thousand acres where these memories grow
From the inexhaustible bodies that are not
Dead, but feed the grass row after rich row.
Think of the autumns that have come and gone!—
Ambitious November with the humours of the year,
With a particular zeal for every slab,
Staining the uncomfortable angels that rot
On the slabs, a wing chipped here, an arm there:
The brute curiosity of an angel's stare
Turns you, like them, to stone,
Transforms the heaving air
Till plunged to a heavier world below
You shift your sea-space blindly
Heaving, turning like a blind crab.

        Dazed by the wind, only the wind
            The leaves flying, plunge

You know who have waited by the wall
The twilight certainty of an animal,
Those midnight restitutions of the blood
You know—the immitigable pines, the smoky frieze
Of the sky, the sudden call: you know the rage,
The cold pool left by the mounting flood,
Of muted Zeno and Parmenides,
You who have waited for the angry resolution
Of those desires that should be yours tomorrow,
You know the unimportant shrift of death
And praise the vision
And praise the arrogant circumstance
Of those who fall

Rank upon rank, hurried beyond decision—
Here by the sagging gate, stopped by the wall.

    Seeing, seeing only the leaves
    Flying, plunge and expire

Turn your eyes to the immoderate past,
Turn to the inscrutable infantry rising
Demons out of the earth—they will not last,
Stonewall, Stonewall, and the sunken fields of hemp,
Shiloh, Antietam, Malvern Hill, Bull Run,
Lost in that orient of the thick-and-fast
You will curse the setting sun.

    Cursing only the leaves crying
    Like an old man in a storm

You hear the shout, the crazy hemlocks point
With troubled fingers to the silence which
Smothers you, a mummy, in time.

    The hound bitch
Toothless and dying, in a musty cellar
Hears the wind only.

    Now that the salt of their blood
Stiffens the saltier oblivion of the sea,
Seals the malignant purity of the flood,
What shall we who count our days and bow
Our heads with a commemorial woe
In the ribboned coats of grim felicity,
What shall we say of the bones, unclean,
Whose verdurous anonymity will grow?

The ragged arms, the ragged heads and eyes
Lost in these acres of the insane green?
The grey lean spiders come, they come and go;
In a tangle of willows without light
The singular screech-owl's tight
Invisible lyric seeds the mind
With the furious murmur of their chivalry.

    We shall say only the leaves
    Flying, plunge and expire

We shall say only the leaves whispering
In the improbable must of nightfall
That flies on multiple wing;
Night is the beginning and the end
And in between the ends of distraction
Waits mute speculation, the patient curse
That stones the eyes, or like the jaguar leaps
For his own image in a jungle pool, his victim.
What shall we say who have knowledge
Carried to the heart? Shall we take the act
To the grave? Shall we, more hopeful, set up the grave
In the house? The ravenous grave?

                         Leave now
The shut gate and the decomposing wall:
The gentle serpent, green in the mulberry bush,
Riots with his tongue through the hush—
Sentinel of the grave who counts us all!

Stephen Spender

SEASCAPE

In Memoriam, M.A.S.

There are some days the happy ocean lies
Like an unfingered harp, below the land.
Afternoon gilds all the silent wires
Into a burning music for the eyes.
On mirrors flashing between fine-strung fires
The shore, heaped up with roses, horses, spires,
Wanders on water, walking above ribbed sand.

The motionlessness of the hot sky tires
And a sigh, like a woman's from inland
Brushes the instrument with shadowing hand
Drawing across its wires some gull's sharp cries
Or bell, or shout, from distant, hedged-in shires;
These, deep as anchors, the hushing wave buries.

Then from the shore, two zig-zag butterflies,
Like errant dog-roses, cross the bright strand
Spiralling over sea in foolish gyres
Until they fall into reflected skies.
They drown. Fishermen understand
Such wings sunk in such ritual sacrifice,

Recalling legends of undersea, drowned cities.
What voyagers, oh what heroes, flamed like pyres
With helmets plumed, have set forth from some island
And them the sea engulfed. Their eyes,
Contorted by the cruel waves' desires
Glitter with coins through the tide scarcely scanned,
While, above them, that harp assumes their sighs.

Robert Lowell

THE QUAKER GRAVEYARD IN NANTUCKET

(For Warren Winslow, Dead at Sea)

Let man have dominion over the fishes of the sea and the fowls of the air and the beasts and the whole earth, and every creeping creature that moveth upon the earth.

I

A brackish reach of shoal off Madaket,—
The sea was still breaking violently and night
Had steamed into our North Atlantic Fleet,
When the drowned sailor clutched the drag-net. Light
Flashed from his matted head and marble feet,
He grappled at the net
With the coiled, hurdling muscles of his thighs:
The corpse was bloodless, a botch of reds and whites,
Its open, staring eyes
Were lustreless dead-lights
Or cabin-windows on a stranded hulk
Heavy with sand. We weight the body, close
Its eyes and heave it seaward whence it came,
Where the heel-headed dogfish barks its nose
On Ahab's void and forehead; and the name
Is blocked in yellow chalk.
Sailors, who pitch this portent at the sea

Where dreadnaughts shall confess
Its hell-bent deity,
When you are powerless

To sandbag this Atlantic bulwark, faced
By the earth-shaker, green, unwearied, chaste
In his steel scales: ask for no Orphean lute
To pluck life back. The guns of the steeled fleet
Recoil and then repeat
The hoarse salute.

II

Whenever winds are moving and their breath
Heaves at the roped-in bulwarks of this pier,
The terns and sea-gulls tremble at your death
In these home waters. Sailor, can you hear
The Pequod's sea wings, beating landward, fall
Headlong and break on our Atlantic wall
Off 'Sconset, where the yawing S-boats splash
The bellbuoy, with ballooning spnnakers,
As the entangled, screeching mainsheet clears
The blocks: off Madaket, where lubbers lash
The heavy surf and throw their long lead squids
For blue-fish? Sea-gulls blink their heavy lids
Seaward. The winds' wings beat upon the stones,
Cousin, and scream for you and the claws rush
At the sea's throat and wring it in the slush
Of this old Quaker graveyard where the bones
Cry out in the long night for the hurt beast
Bobbing by Ahab's whaleboats in the East.

III

All you recovered from Poseidon died
With you, my cousin, and the harrowed brine
Is fruitless on the blue beard of the god,
Stretching beyond us to the castles in Spain,
Nantucket's westward haven. To Cape Cod

Guns, cradled on the tide,
Blast the eelgrass about a waterlock
Of bilge and backwash, roil the salt and sand
Lashing earth's scaffold, rock
Our warships in the hand
Of the great God, where time's contrition blues
Whatever it was these Quaker sailors lost
In the mad scramble of their lives. They died
When time was open-eyed,
Wooden and childish; only bones abide
There, in the nowhere, where their boats were tossed
Sky-high, where mariners had fabled news
Of IS, the whited monster. What it cost
Them is their secret. In the sperm whale's slick
I see the Quakers drown and hear their cry:
'If God himself had not been on our side,
If God himself had not been on our side,
When the Atlantic rose against us, why,
Then it had swallowed us up quick.'

IV

This is the end of the whaleroad and the whale
Who spewed Nantucket bones on the thrashed swell
And stirred the troubled waters to whirlpools
To send the Pequod packing off to hell:
This is the end of them, three-quarters fools,
Snatching at straws to sail
Seaward and seaward on the turntail whale,
Spouting out blood and water as it rolls,
Sick as a dog to these Atlantic shoals:
Clamavimus, O depths. Let the sea-gulls wail

For water, for the deep where the high tide
Mutters to its hurt self, mutters and ebbs.

Waves wallow in their wash, go out and out,
Leave only the death-rattle of the crabs,
The beach increasing, its enormous snout
Sucking the ocean's side.
This is the end of running on the waves;
We are poured out like water. Who will dance
The mast-lashed master of Leviathans
Up from this field of Quakers in their unstoned graves?

V

When the whale's viscera go and the roll
Of its corruption overruns this world
Beyond tree-swept Nantucket and Wood's Hole
And Martha's Vineyard, Sailor, will your sword
Whistle and fall and sink into the fat?
In the great ash-pit of Jehoshaphat
The bones cry for the blood of the white whale,
The fat flukes arch and whack about its ears,
The death-lance churns into the sanctuary, tears
The gun-blue swingle, heaving like a flail,
And hacks the coiling life out: it works and drags
And rips the sperm-whale's midriff into rags,
Gobbets of blubber spill to wind and weather,
Sailor, and gulls go round the stoven timbers
Where the morning stars sing out together
And thunder shakes the white surf and dismembers
The red flag hammered in the mast-head. Hide,
Our steel, Jonah Messiah, in Thy side.

VI

OUR LADY OF WALSINGHAM

There once the penitents took off their shoes
And then walked barefoot the remaining mile;

And the small trees, a stream and hedgerows file
Slowly along the munching English lane,
Like cows to the old shrine, until you lose
Track of your dragging pain.
The stream flows down under the druid tree,
Shiloah's whirlpools gurgle and make glad
The castle of God. Sailor, you were glad
And whistled Sion by that stream. But see:

Our Lady, too small for her canopy,
Sits near the altar. There's no comeliness
At all or charm in that expressionless
Face with its heavy eyelids. As before,
This face, for centuries a memory,
Non est species, neque decor,
Expressionless, expresses God: it goes
Past castled Sion. She knows what God knows.
Not Calvary's Cross nor crib at Bethlehem
Now, and the world shall come to Walsingham.

VII

The empty winds are creaking and the oak
Splatters and splatters on the cenotaph,
The boughs are trembling and a gaff
Bobs on the untimely stroke
Of the greased wash exploding on a shoal-bell
In the old mouth of the Atlantic. It's well;
Atlantic, you are fouled with the blue sailors,
Sea-monsters, upward angel, downward fish:
Unmarried and corroding, spare of flesh,
Mart once of supercilious, wing'd clippers,
Atlantic, where your bell-trap guts its spoil
You could cut the brackish winds with a knife
Here in Nantucket, and cast up the time

When the Lord God formed man from the sea's slime
And breathed into his face the breath of life,
And blue-lung'd combers lumbered to the kill.
The Lord survives the rainbow of His will.

Richard Eberhart

THE FURY OF AERIAL BOMBARDMENT

You would think the fury of aerial bombardment
Would rouse God to relent; the infinite spaces
Are still silent. He looks on shock-pried faces.
History, even, does not know what is meant.

You would feel that after so many centuries
God would give man to repent; yet he can kill
As Cain could, but with multitudinous will,
No farther advanced than in his ancient furies.

Was man made stupid to see his own stupidity?
Is God by definition indifferent, beyond us all?
Is the eternal truth man's fighting soul
Wherein the Beast ravens in its own avidity?

Of Van Wettering I speak, and Averill,
Names on a list, whose faces I do not recall
But they are gone to early death, who late in school
Distinguished the belt feed lever from the belt holding pawl.

Richard Wilbur
ADVICE TO A PROPHET

When you come, as you soon must, to the streets of our city,
Mad-eyed from stating the obvious,
Not proclaiming our fall but begging us
In God's name to have self-pity,

Spare us all word of the weapons, their force and range,
The long numbers that rocket the mind;
Our slow, unreckoning hearts will be left behind,
Unable to fear what is too strange.

Nor shall you scare us with talk of the death of the race.
How should we dream of this place without us—
The sun mere fire, the leaves untroubled about us,
A stone look on the stone's face?

Speak of the world's own change. Though we cannot conceive
Of an undreamt thing, we know to our cost
How the dreamt cloud crumbles, the vines are blackened by
        frost,
How the view alters. We could believe,

If you told us so, that the white-tailed deer will slip
Into perfect shade, grown perfectly shy,
The lark avoid the reaches of our eye,
The jack-pine lose its knuckled grip.

On the cold ledge, and every torrent burn
As Xanthus once, its gliding trout
Stunned in a twinkling. What should we be without
The dolphin's arc, the dove's return,

These things in which we have seen ourselves and spoken?
Ask us, prophet, how we shall call
Our natures forth when that live tongue is all
Dispelled, that glass obscured or broken,

In which we have said the rose of our love and the clean
Horse of our courage, in which beheld
The singing locust of the soul unshelled,
And all we mean or wish to mean.

Ask us, ask us whether with the worldless rose
Our hearts shall fail us; come demanding
Whether there shall be lofty or long standing
When the bronze annals of the oak-tree close.

Louis MacNeice

BROTHER FIRE

When our brother Fire was having his dog's day
Jumping the London streets with millions of tin cans
Clanking at his tail, we heard some shadow say
'Give the dog a bone'—and so we gave him ours;
Night after night we watched him slaver and crunch away
The beams of human life, the tops of topless towers.

Which gluttony of his for us was Lenten fare
Who mother-naked, suckled with sparks, were chill
Though cotted in a grill of sizzling air
Striped like a convict—black, yellow and red;
Thus were we weaned to knowledge of the Will
That wills the natural world but wills us dead.

O delicate walker, babbler, dialectician Fire,
O enemy and image of ourselves,
Did we not on those mornings after the All Clear,
When you were looting shops in elemental joy
And singing as you swarmed up city block and spire,
Echo your thought in ours? 'Destroy! Destroy!'

Dylan Thomas

A REFUSAL TO MOURN THE DEATH, BY FIRE, OF A CHILD IN LONDON

Never until the mankind making
Bird beast and flower
Fathering and all humbling darkness
Tells with silence the last light breaking
And the still hour
Is come of the sea tumbling in harness

And I must enter again the round
Zion of the water bead
And the synagogue of the ear of corn
Shall I let pray the shadow of a sound
Or sow my salt seed
In the least valley of sackcloth to mourn

The majesty and burning of the child's death.
I shall not murder
The mankind of her going with a grave truth
Nor blaspheme down the stations of the breath
With any further
Elegy of innocence and youth.

Deep with the first dead lies London's daughter,
Robed in the long friends,
The grains beyond age, the dark veins of her mother,
Secret by the unmourning water
Of the riding Thames.
After the first death, there is no other.

William Carlos Williams

TRACT

I will teach you my townspeople
how to perform a funeral—
for you have it over a troop
of artists—
unless one should scour the world—
you have the ground sense necessary.

See! the hearse leads.
I begin with a design for a hearse.
For Christ's sake not black—
nor white either—and not polished!
Let it be weathered—like a farm wagon—
with gilt wheels (this could be
applied fresh at small expense)
or no wheels at all:
a rough dray to drag over the ground.

Knock the glass out!
My God—glass, my townspeople!
For what purpose? Is it for the dead
to look out or for us to see

how well he is housed or to see
the flowers or the lack of them—
or what?
To keep the rain and snow from him?
He will have a heavier rain soon:
pebbles and dirt and what not.
Let there be no glass—
and no upholstery phew!
and no little brass rollers
and small easy wheels on the bottom—
my townspeople what are you thinking of?

A rough plain hearse then
with gilt wheels and no top at all.
On this the coffin lies
by its own weight.

No wreaths please—
especially no hot-house flowers.
Some common memento is better,
something he prized and is known by:
his old clothes—a few books perhaps—
God knows what! You realize
how we are about these things
my townspeople—
something will be found—anything
even flowers if he had come to that.
So much for the hearse.

For heaven's sake though see to the driver!
Take off the silk hat! In fact
that's no place at all for him—
up there unceremoniously
dragging our friend out to his own dignity!
Bring him down—bring him down!

Low and inconspicuous! I'd not have him ride
on the wagon at all—damn him—
the undertaker's understrapper!
Let him hold the reins
and walk at the side
and inconspicuously too!

Then briefly as to yourselves:
Walk behind—as they do in France,
seventh class, or if you ride
Hell take curtains! Go with some show
of inconvenience; sit openly—
to the weather as to grief.
Or do you think you can shut grief in?
What—from us? We who have perhaps
nothing to lose? Share with us
share with us—it will be money
in your pockets.
        Go now
I think you are ready.

Gerard Manley Hopkins

FELIX RANDAL

Felix Randal the farrier, O he is dead then? my duty all
        ended,
Who have watched his mould of man, big-boned and
        hardy-handsome
Pining, pining, till time when reason rambled in it and
        some
Fatal four disorders, fleshed there, all contended?

Sickness broke him. Impatient he cursed at first, but
  mended
Being anointed and all; though a heavenlier heart began
  some
Months earlier, since I had our sweet reprieve and ransom
Tendered to him. Ah well, God rest him all road ever he
  offended!

This seeing the sick endears them to us, us too it endears.
My tongue had taught thee comfort, touch had quenched
  thy tears,
Thy tears that touched my heart, child, Felix, poor
  Felix Randal;

How far from then forethought of, all thy more boisterous
  years,
When thou at the random grim forge, powerful amidst
  peers,
Didst fettle for the great grey drayhorse his bright and
  battering sandal!

Thomas Hardy
DRUMMER HODGE

They throw in Drummer Hodge, to rest
  Uncoffined—just as found:
His landmark is a kopje-crest
  That breaks the veldt around;
And foreign constellations west
  Each night above his mound.

Young Hodge the Drummer never knew—
    Fresh from his Wessex home—
The meaning of the broad Karoo,
    The Bush, the dusty loam,
And why uprose to nightly view
    Strange stars amid the gloam.

Yet portion of that unknown plain
    Will Hodge for ever be;
His homely Northern breast and brain
    Grow to some Southern tree,
And strange-eyed constellations reign
    His stars eternally.

Lawrence Durrell

NEMEA

A song in the valley of Nemea:
Sing quiet, quite quiet here.

Song for the brides of Argos
Combing the swarms of golden hair:
Quite quiet, quiet there.

Under the rolling comb of grass,
The sword outrusts the golden helm.

Agamemnon under tumulus serene
Outsmiles the jury of skeletons:
Cool under cumulus the lion queen:

Only the drum can celebrate,
Only the adjective outlive them.

A song in the valley of Nemea:
Sing quiet, quiet, quiet here.

Tone of the frog in the empty well,
Drone of the bald bee on the cold skull,

Quiet, Quiet, Quiet.

Geoffrey Hill

REQUIEM FOR THE PLANTAGENET KINGS

For whom the possessed sea littered, on both shores,
Ruinous arms; being fired, and for good,
To sound the constitution of just wars,
Men, in their eloquent fashion, understood.

Relieved of soul, the dropping-back of dust,
Their usage, pride, admitted within doors;
At home, under caved chantries, set in trust,
With well-dressed alabaster and proved spurs
They lie; they lie; secure in the decay
Of blood, blood-marks, crowns hacked and coveted,
Before the scouring fires of trial-day
Alight on men; before sleeked groin, gored head,
Budge through the clay and gravel, and the sea
Across daubed rock evacuates its dead.

Lawrence Durrell
EPITAPH

Here lies Michael of the small bone.
The pride of the lion is gone home.
God lend our England such a one.

A knight's memoriam is only love.
So Michael with his dog on his leg
To his sweet Vicar is gone above.

His loyalty was better than the people's mud.
His going down on the jaw of the common dog,
This was a godly fellow's manœuvre.

His breath as pure as the great oven of Mary.
He spoke to God with the tongue of great bell.
They taste his humour at the centre of the world.

Michael the Englishman of the small bone,
Simple and pure as water in a spoon,
God lend our England such a one.

C. A. Trypanis
PICTURE OF THE NATIVITY IN THE CHURCH OF KRENA IN CHIOS

—Tell me, can this unsuspecting infant, staring
At the steep green sky, be 'He, who trampled upon Death'?
Everything round him is so poor and so untrue,

The brown ponies like shabby toys, the shepherds stilted
On their crooks, the Magi wooden kings that dare not bend,
Even the angels, village angels—they could never
Reach the sky again with those flat, clumsy wings.

—Silently, unawares and unbelievably come all
Great things: the inroad of great love, the mist of death.

Philip Larkin
CHURCH GOING

Once I am sure there's nothing going on
I step inside, letting the door thud shut.
Another church: matting, seats, and stone,
And little books; sprawlings of flowers, cut
For Sunday, brownish now; some brass and stuff
Up at the holy end; the small neat organ;
And a tense, musty, unignorable silence,
Brewed God knows how long. Hatless, I take off
My cycle-clips in awkward reverence,

Move forward, run my hand around the font.
From where I stand, the roof looks almost new—
Cleaned, or restored? Someone would know: I don't.
Mounting the lectern, I peruse a few
Hectoring large-scale verses, and pronounce
'Here endeth' much more loudly than I'd meant.
The echoes snigger briefly. Back at the door
I sign the book, donate an Irish sixpence,
Reflect the place was not worth stopping for.

Yet stop I did: in fact I often do,
And always end much at a loss like this,
Wondering what to look for; wondering, too,
When churches fall completely out of use
What we shall turn them into, if we shall keep
A few cathedrals chronically on show,
Their parchment, plate and pyx in locked cases,
And let the rest rent-free to rain and sheep.
Shall we avoid them as unlucky places?

Or, after dark, will dubious women come
To make their children touch a particular stone;
Pick simples for a cancer; or on some
Advised night see walking a dead one?
Power of some sort or other will go on
In games, in riddles, seemingly at random;
But superstition, like belief, must die,
And what remains when disbelief has gone?
Grass, weedy pavement, brambles, buttress, sky,

A shape less recognizable each week,
A purpose more obscure. I wonder who
Will be the last, the very last, to seek
This place for what it was; one of the crew
That tap and jot and know what rood-lofts were?
Some ruin-bibber, randy for antique,
Or Christmas-addict, counting on a whiff
Of gown-and-bands and organ-pipes and myrrh?
Or will he be my representative,

Bored, uninformed, knowing the ghostly silt
Dispersed, yet tending to this cross of ground
Through suburb scrub because it held unspilt
So long and equably what since is found
Only in separation—marriage, and birth,

And death, and thoughts of these—for whom was built
This special shell? For, though I've no idea
What this accountred frowsty barn is worth,
It pleases me to stand in silence here;

A serious house on serious earth it is,
In whose blent air all our compulsions meet,
Are recognized, and robed as destinies.
And that much never can be obsolete,
Since someone will forever be surprising
A hunger in himself to be more serious,
And gravitating with it to this ground,
Which, he once heard, was proper to grow wise in,
If only that so many dead lie round.

*   *

Editor's Note: At this point I had intended to print the famous
'terza rima' section from T. S. Eliot's *Little Gidding*, i.e. the whole
of Section 2 of the poem except for the lyric, 'Ash on an old
man's sleeve', with which the section begins. In this passage,
beginning 'In the uncertain hour before the morning' and end-
ing 'And faded on the blowing of the horn', we have the perfect
counterpart to *Gerontion* (printed on pp. 131–4), in that both
poems deal with the problems of old age, and the later one
carries the subject considerably further.

It seems, however, that Mr Eliot makes a firm rule not to
allow any of the *Four Quartets*, of which *Little Gidding* is the fourth,
to be printed piecemeal; the only parts he will allow an anthologist to extract are the lyrics, of which each Quartet contains one, and which have (perhaps in consequence) been over-
anthologized already, in my opinion. The section from *Little
Gidding* cannot, therefore, be printed here. But anyone wishing
to get the fullest use from this book will take down the poem
and read that passage, at this point; it is to be found in any of
the Collected editions of Mr Eliot's poems; and the reader who

is sufficiently interested in twentieth-century poetry to be using this anthology will surely have, or have access to, some such edition.

*　　*

William Empson
MISSING DATES

Slowly the poison the whole blood stream fills.
It is not the effort nor the failure tires.
The waste remains, the waste remains and kills.

It is not your system or clear sight that mills
Down small to the consequence a life requires;
Slowly the poison the whole blood stream fills.

They bled an old dog dry yet the exchange rills
Of young dog blood gave but a month's desires;
The waste remains, the waste remains and kills.

It is the Chinese tombs and the slag hills
Usurp the soil, and not the soil retires.
Slowly the poison the whole blood stream fills.

Not to have fire is to be a skin that shrills.
The complete fire is death. From partial fires
The waste remains, the waste remains and kills.

It is the poems you have lost, the ills
From missing dates, at which the heart expires.
Slowly the poison the whole blood stream fills.
The waste remains, the waste remains and kills.

W. B. Yeats

TO A FRIEND WHOSE WORK HAS COME TO NOTHING

Now all the truth is out,
Be secret and take defeat
From any brazen throat,
For how can you compete,
Being honour bred, with one
Who, were it proved he lies,
Were neither shamed in his own
Nor in his neighbours' eyes?
Bred to a harder thing
Than Triumph, turn away
And like a laughing string
Whereon mad fingers play
Amid a place of stone,
Be secret and exult,
Because of all things known
That is most difficult.

Dylan Thomas

DO NOT GO GENTLE INTO THAT GOOD NIGHT

Do not go gentle into that good night,
Old age should burn and rave at close of day;
Rage, rage against the dying of the light.

Though wise men at their end know dark is right,
Because their words had forked no lightning they
Do not go gentle into that good night.

Good men, the last wave by, crying how bright
Their frail deeds might have danced in a green bay,
Rage, rage against the dying of the light.

Wild men who caught and sang the sun in flight,
And learn, too late, they grieved it on its way,
Do not go gentle into that good night.

Grave men, near death, who see with blinding sight
Blind eyes could blaze like meteors and be gay,
Rage, rage against the dying of the light.

And you, my father, there on the sad height,
Curse, bless, me now with your fierce tears, I pray.
Do not go gentle into that good night.
Rage, rage against the dying of the light.

Ezra Pound

Δώρια

Be in me as the eternal moods
  of the bleak wind, and not
As transient things are—
  gaiety of flowers.
Have me in the strong loneliness
  of sunless cliffs
And of greywaters.
  Let the gods speak softly of us
In days hereafter,
  The shadowy flowers of Orcus
Remember thee.

Gerard Manley Hopkins
NO WORST, THERE IS NONE

No worst, there is none. Pitched past pitch of grief,
More pangs will, schooled at forepangs, wilder wring.
Comforter, where, where is your comforting?
Mary, mother of us, where is your relief?
My cries heave, herds-long; huddle in a main, a chief
Woe, world-sorrow; on an age-old anvil wince and sing—
Then lull, then leave off. Fury had shrieked 'No linger-
    ing! Let me be fell: force I must be brief'.

  O the mind, mind has mountains; cliffs of fall
Frightful, sheer, no-man-fathomed. Hold them cheap
May who ne'er hung there. Nor does long our small
Durance deal with that steep or deep. Here! creep,
Wretch, under a comfort serves in a whirlwind: all
Life death does end and each day dies with sleep.

Thomas Hardy
AFTERWARDS

When the Present has latched its postern behind my tremulous
    stay,
  And the May month flaps its glad green leaves like wings,
Delicate-filmed as new-spun silk, will the neighbours say,
  'He was a man who used to notice such things'?

If it be in the dusk when, like an eyelid's soundless blink,
  The dewfall-hawk comes crossing the shades to alight

Upon the wind-warped upland thorn, a gazer may think,
    'To him this must have been a familiar sight.'

If I pass during some nocturnal blackness, mothy and warm,
    When the hedgehog travels furtively over the lawn,
One may say, 'He strove that such innocent creatures should
        come to no harm,
    But he could do little for them; and now he is gone.'

If, when hearing that I have been stilled at last, they stand at the
        door,
    Watching the full-starred heavens that winter sees,
Will this thought rise on those who will meet my face no more
    'He was one who had an eye for such mysteries'?

And will any say when my bell of quittance is heard in the
        gloom,
    And a crossing breeze cuts a pause in its outrollings,
Till they rise again, as they were a new bell's boom,
    'He hears it not now, but used to notice such things'?

W. B. Yeats

A PRAYER FOR OLD AGE

God guard me from those thoughts men think
In the mind alone;
He that sings a lasting song
Thinks in a marrow-bone;

From all that makes a wise old man
That can be praised of all;

O what am I that I should not seem
For the song's sake a fool?

I pray—for fashion's word is out
And prayer comes round again—
That I may seem, though I die old,
A foolish, passionate man.

Commentary

W. H. AUDEN, b. 1907

For general comment see Introduction, *passim*. Auden's COL-
LECTED SHORTER POEMS (1950) contains the bulk of his work
up to that date, but there has been much since. His lively and
wide-ranging taste makes him a skilled anthologist, and a good
deal can be learnt about his attitudes from two anthologies he
has compiled, THE OXFORD BOOK OF LIGHT VERSE (1938) and
THE FABER BOOK OF MODERN AMERICAN VERSE (1955). His
best critical book is the fascinating THE ENCHAFÈD FLOOD
(1950).

Consider this and in our time (p. 40) is typical of Auden's 'nagging'
poems of the 1930's. Under the apparent prosperity, the game is
up: the 'supreme Antagonist'—some indefinable phantom of
defeat and destruction—will smash the society to pieces and
scatter the people, and the troops who will win this victory for
him are, of course, 'the ill'—those whom boredom and emptiness have drained of true human feelings.

Will you turn a deaf ear (p. 50) handles the same theme, though
it is far more opaque in style. I had better confess at once that I
could not, with any confidence, give a prose paraphrase of this
poem. The well-bred neurotics in their rich houses are, as
usual, the agents by means of whom Death is let loose. The
rescuer will behave with perfect propriety, saluting the flag and
not belonging to illegal organizations; but he will strike his blow
against the 'neutralizing peace and average disgrace'—a phrase
which sums up the quality of life in England during the late
1930's. In general, this poem is far from satisfactory; Henry
Reed once wrote of Auden, 'His early verse was usually too

obscure to give complete satisfaction, but its freshness and gusto and assurance had given one a good deal to delight in.' All those qualities are here; as an adolescent, I delighted in this and similar poems of Auden's which seemed to speak to me directly by their tone and rhythm, seemed to be of my world when so much of the verse I read was not; and I therefore include it here.

Thechorus which ends *Paid on Both Sides* (p. 83)—an early dramatic piece which Auden described as 'a charade'—shows Auden's extraordinary mastery, even in his early days, of tone and form. It is obviously much influenced, in its laconic heaviness and terseness, by the Anglo-Saxon poetry he read as a student at Oxford: but Anglo-Saxon poetry has no rhymes, and these lines are in a kind of rhymed chant which could easily be spoken by a chorus of several voices.

ROY CAMPBELL, 1902–1957

A South African poet, Roy Campbell spent some years in London, where he clashed violently with many of the established literary figures and satirized them in a long, uneconomical but amusing poem, *The Georgiad* (1931). Like Ernest Hemingway, Campbell had a need for physical action and violence, which he satisfied to the full in a life of fishing, bull-fighting and soldiering. Growing up in a stark, dramatic tropical setting, he was never at home with the soft greens and greys of England— climatic or personal—and his European sympathies come out best in his translations of Portuguese and Spanish poetry, especially his translation of the poems of the Spanish mystic St John of the Cross, where his religious feelings (he was a Roman Catholic) combine with his deep sense of the Spanish temperament. He was killed in a motor accident in 1957.

Autumn (p. 80) is a poem that contains the essence of Campbell's attitude to art as well as to nature.

The Zulu Girl (p. 93) is the best-known of the many poems he wrote about primitive people, whose bodily needs dictate the pattern of their lives; Campbell deeply respected such people and detested anyone he considered over-civilized.

E. E. CUMMINGS, 1894–1962 (U.S.A.)

A veteran modernist, Cummings was interested from the beginning in typographical arrangements which indicate how the poem should be spoken aloud, so that his poetry often looks odd on the page, much odder than it sounds. He was also interested in the creative dislocation of grammar, whereby one part of speech does duty for another. *My Father moved through Dooms of Love* (p. 134) will repay study along these lines.

After serving in the First World War (where, owing to some official's error, he spent three months in a French internment camp—an experience he recounted unforgettably in THE ENORMOUS ROOM, 1922) Cummings studied painting in Paris. His highly developed visual sense is very evident in his writing; many of his poems seem like Cubist paintings put into words.

BABETTE DEUTSCH, b. 1895 (U.S.A.)

A poet whose work should be better known in England (there is a convenient selection in COMING OF AGE, 1960), Babette Deutsch has a simplicity of style which is deceptive; always elegant, her poetry is never *merely* so.

Young Gazelle (p. 72) comes from a sequence, *Creatures in the Zoo*, which should be read in full.

LAWRENCE DURRELL, b. 1912

Of Irish descent, born in India, Durrell has passed much of his life in Mediterranean countries, particularly Greece and Egypt (cf. his enormous novel-sequence, THE ALEXANDRIA QUARTET). His poetry is distinguished both by a highly personal music— he is one of the very few successful *lyric* poets now writing—and by the sharp precision of its visual imagery.

Green Man (p. 59) is 'about' nothing except the poet sitting writing at a table while his wife reads in the same room. Since what he is writing is a poem, it gives him the sensation of creating the universe freshly, or at least of naming the animals like Adam. Even the giant tortoise who, in Hindu mythology, carries the world on his back has a special verb assigned to him.

To Ping-Kû, Asleep (p. 89) appears to me to need no commentary except to point out that Ping-Kû is a pet name for the poet's baby daughter, and that a nautilus is a creature of the same kind as an octopus: the child lies asleep with the tentacles of her parents' love branching out all round.

Dmitri of Carpathos (p. 122) is a comic vignette which turns into a statement about the relationship between a sailor, even a good-for-nothing sailor, and his boat.

Epitaph (p. 167), a meditation on one of those chipped medieval crusaders one comes across in English churches, seems to me a perfect small-scale achievement, though the poet did not think it worth including in his COLLECTED POEMS (1960).

RICHARD EBERHART, b. 1904 (U.S.A.)

Born in Minnesota, Richard Eberhart was educated in America and England, was tutor for a year to the son of King Prajadhipok of Siam, served in the U.S. Naval Reserve as an aircraft gunnery instructor, has been a business man (with the Butcher Polish Company of Boston, Mass.) and a professor at several universities, and has also served as Poetry Consultant at the Library of Congress in Washington, D.C. His varied and energetic life comes through in his poetry, which is rugged, inquisitive and forceful; clumsy in patches, supremely felicitous in others. The poems I have selected (pp. 63, 143, 157) need no annotation, I feel.

T. S. ELIOT, 1888–1965

No single poet has been more important in the development of modern poetry, all over the English-speaking world and beyond it, than Thomas Stearns Eliot, in whose mind the gifts of the poet and the critic met and mingled in an extraordinarily rich way. His great influence has been abundantly recognized, by such honours as the award of the Nobel Prize for Literature and the Order of Merit; and also by the unforced tributes paid to him by scores of poets younger than himself.

Mr Eliot, though his birthplace was St Louis, Missouri, actually came of a New England family. After an elaborate education— at Harvard, Oxford and Paris—he settled in England in 1915 and took British nationality in 1927. After a brief spell in the foreign department of Lloyds Bank, he became director of a well-known publishing house, and worked there for the rest of his life.

Eliot's originality, and his determination to strike out a new idiom in English poetry, were at once apparent in his first book, PRUFROCK AND OTHER OBSERVATIONS (1917). In 1920 he brought out his first critical work, THE SACRED WOOD; these essays have long since been merged in Eliot's various collected and selected volumes, but the excitement of the original publication is worth savouring on its own, and copies are easily available. Two years later came his most controversial poetic work, THE WASTE LAND, which became the battleground of a generation. In 1936 Mr Eliot gathered his earlier poems in COLLECTED POEMS 1909–1935, and in 1944 he published FOUR QUARTETS, a major four-part religious and philosophical poem whose composition had largely occupied the intervening years. Since then he has devoted himself mainly to writing verse plays, in which his interest can be traced from the beginning of his career.

Anyone with an interest in modern poetry will read Eliot entire, and I have quailed before the impossible task of representing his work in all its gigantic importance.

Gerontion (p. 131) is one of Eliot's earlier poems, published in 1920, and reflects his intense interest at that time in the Elizabethan and Jacobean writers, and particularly the dramatists. The verse rhythms, while never suggesting this or that individual writer, are modelled on the general pattern of the dramatic verse of the period, contriving simultaneously to remind us of Webster, Tourneur, Marston and even Shakespeare, whose MEASURE FOR MEASURE provides the epigraph. γερων is Greek for an old man, and *Gerontion* means either a little poem about an old man, or a poem about a little old man. Probably the latter. The poem opens with the boredom and discontent of the old man, whom life has passed by, leaving him 'waiting for rain'. The rain he looks for is a symbol of renewed life (as in Hopkins's desperate cry, 'Mine, O thou lord of life, send my roots rain'). It soon becomes clear that the inspiration he half longs for, half fears, is religious in character. In May, which is 'depraved' because it is flaunting and sensual, Christ leaps like a tiger: this is not the sentimentalized figure of Christ in the magazine supplements at Christmas, but the Saviour who makes all but impossible demands, who destroys that he may save. He is eaten, divided and drunk, i.e. at communion, by—and here we enter one of the passages which people have found baffling—Mr Silvero, Hakagawa, Madame de Tornquist and Fräulein von Kulp. Who are these people, and what are they doing in the poem?

The answer is that they are all symbolic, generalized characters, like the old man himself, the boy, the woman, and the Jewish landlord. Mr Silvero, with his caressing hands and his restlessness: Hakagawa, whose devotion is given to paintings:

Madame de Tornquist, who takes up fortune-telling, and Fräulein von Kulp, her client, are all people in whom the instinct for devotion has become misdirected. They are religious people without a religion, and hence very characteristic of the modern world. The old man meditates upon this until his tears fall; they are shaken from the tree of knowledge, his own knowledge, which in the Book of Genesis is also the tree of the wrath of God. 'I would meet you honestly,' he says to Christ. But his senses, through which illumination comes, have decayed. Christ is as beautiful, and also as terrible, as a leaping tiger; but the old man is beyond perceiving beauty, and he has also (as the passage about 'history' indicates) passed beyond even terror into a continual questioning or 'inquisition'. Close contact seems no longer possible for him; he scorns to keep his senses alive, as some old men do, with sauces and drugs which 'excite the membrane when the sense has cooled'—a line, incidentally, which would not seem surprising in Webster and yet is entirely modern.

Death will destroy everyone, whirling them into the constellations in fractured atoms, including all the people whose names lodge at random in the old man's memory. The trade winds blow the gull off course, and in some snow-flurry it is exhausted and drowned; this will happen to the old man too, but meanwhile the same trade winds—the irresistible forces of history and his own life—have driven him into a sleepy corner, where he waits for release with a sullen patience. These are the poem's main outlines, though a full exploration is impossible for reasons of space.

The section from *Little Gidding*, 1942, which I should have liked to include (see note on p. 170), is to some extent a harking-back to *Gerontion*, though in the richer context provided by the poem and by the Four Quartets in general. Just as *Gerontion* recalls Jacobean poetry, while remaining firmly itself, so this passage recalls Dante's DIVINE COMEDY in its setting, its atmosphere and the movement of its verse. Characteristically, Eliot manages to combine the Dantean flavour, in this account of a meeting with the spirit of a man in purgatory, with a complete faithfulness to the spirit of 1942. The 'I' of the poem is both a visionary wanderer in the realms of spiritual truth, like the 'I' of the DIVINE COMEDY, and, on a prosaic everyday level, an air-raid warden, pacing his allotted stretch of pavement in the last watch of the night, before the dawn but after the departure of the bomber—the 'dark dove with the flickering tongue', which destroys and also brings the peace of death. The purgatorial spirit is evidently that of some teacher of the youthful Eliot; now he tells him—among other things—what to expect from old age. The best hope (and here we have part of the answer to the agonized questioning of *Gerontion*) is in purification through suffering. Purgatorial fire is not meaningless pain; it is made significant by a discipline as strict as that of the dance.

The ghost vanishes on the blowing of a 'horn', which is his summons back to the shades and also, in a perfectly matter-of-fact way, the 'all clear' which means that the warden can go off duty.

WILLIAM EMPSON, b. 1906

A widely influential critic as well as a poet, Empson has taught English literature in China and Japan. He studied mathematics and science at Cambridge, before turning to literature, and has retained a strong interest in these subjects. His early poems reflected his scientific training and his interest in the seventeenth-century 'Metaphysical' poets who incorporated ideas from science and theology in their work; his later poems, while still showing the same fierce intellectual curiosity, are easier to understand and more concerned with the business of day-to-day living. He returned to England from China in 1952, and now lives between Hampstead, where he has a house, and Sheffield, where he is Professor of English Literature.

William Empson's COLLECTED POEMS came out in 1955, and

he has written very little verse since then. Many valuable clues to the understanding of his poetry can be found in his own critical works, particularly the famous SEVEN TYPES OF AMBIGUITY (1931); and his general attitudes are summed up, along the way, in his wide-ranging and controversial MILTON'S GOD (1961).

To an Old Lady (p. 130), which I understand describes the poet's mother, seems to me the best example of that modern 'metaphysical' poetry which arose in the 'twenties and 'thirties as a result of the renewed interest in Donne's poetry and the feeling that poets ought to enlarge the range of their verse so as to bring in present-day intellectual developments, including science. The 'meaning' of this poem, put quite simply, is: 'My mother, rooted in a generation whose ways are not mine, is very strange to me, as strange as the things scientists tell me about distant planets. The only way to find out about life on these planets is to observe, not to go there, which would be to risk appearing a blundering intruder; in the same way, I cannot intervene in the old lady's life, but must be content to observe from a distance. When I observe her, I find many of her resources going to waste, as a planet's might (*appanage*: originally the arrangements made for the support of the younger children of kings, hence perquisite, resources); her wit has found no other outlet than dinners and bridge-parties, her tragic fervour, which could have risen to great occasions, found nothing greater to rise to than the dismissal of a servant now and then. Still, her confidence and solidity are wonderful. Just as the stars are invisible in daylight, so the fact that she inhabits the same world as I do ('shares my sun') only makes her harder to understand.' In its combination of spry, tough intellectual alertness with brooding tenderness, this poem seems to me a masterpiece.

Missing Dates (p. 171), is in Empson's later, simpler manner. In his own note on the poem, he mentions that the story about renewing the dog's blood is true, but the statement that a fifth of the soil of China is given over to ancestral tombs is not.

Manchouli (p. 49) dates from the time when Empson took a job in China in 1937, a few weeks after the Chinese had been attacked by Japan. Manchouli (its English name is 'Lupin') is a town on the Siberian border, the sort of big frontier town where hopeless refugees cluster and exist for years: this (as the poem so tellingly says) is what our callousness has come to call 'normal'—yet without this callousness we probably could not live at all.

ROBERT GRAVES, b. 1895

Two prose best-sellers (GOODBYE TO ALL THAT, 1929, and I, CLAUDIUS, 1934) overshadowed Robert Graves's achievement as a poet during the inter-war years, and it was not until the publication of his COLLECTED POEMS in 1948 that his poetic reputation, which had been growing among poets for some time, moved clearly into focus for the reading public at large. A delicate and spare lyricism, a quizzical wit, an occasional mordant irony, a scholarly use of language—these are the usual marks of a Graves poem. In addition, he is deeply interested in myth and symbolism, studying legend, folk-tale and religion for their clues to the real nature of man's mind. Graves's scholarship is undeniable, and he has intervened in a number of discussions among professors, always with disconcerting results, for he has an impish love of the preposterous thesis and the 'shocking' sidelight. The most serious of his attacks on en-trenched scholarly opinion was made in THE NAZARENE GOSPELS RESTORED, in which he put forward a highly un-orthodox view of the origins of Christianity. There is also much that is personal in Graves's two-volume Pelican, THE GREEK MYTHS (1955). His life has been eventful; among other things he has been an infantry officer (in some of the bitterest fighting of the First World War), lived in Majorca on and off since 1929, fathered eight children, kept a grocer's shop and been Professor of Poetry at Oxford.

Mermaid, Dragon, Fiend (p. 65) expresses Graves's belief that monsters and horrors are not outside ourselves, to be faced and routed as the knights of old slew dragons, but inside, part of our human nature: the struggle, which can never be finally won but must always be renewed, takes place in the silence of our own hearts. This is by no means Graves's only poem on this theme: *Saint* (p. 125) is another.

Outlaws (p. 70) reflects the poet's feeling for myth, legends, superstition, and the things they can teach us about man's mind. Have you ever felt scared in a wood at night? Does this poem help to make clear to you the nature of what was happening inside you?

Recalling War (p. 137) reminds us that Graves is a contemporary of Wilfred Owen's. This magnificent poem distils the essence of Graves's thought about the experience, mental and physical, of warfare.

The Suicide in the Copse (p. 119) tried to solve his problems by running away from life, and succeeded only in falling into worse boredom, worse emptiness. Notice the aptness of the verse-form to what is being said, here and in all Graves's poems.

Ancestors (p. 82) represents both the fanciful side of Graves and also his impatient individualism. The ghosts of his ancestors are welcome to drink mulled wine with him on New Year's Eve—till they become boastful and boring, insist too much on their own importance, and he rejects them. Do you ever imagine the ghosts of your ancestors? Is the average ghost-story a true reflection of the ways one can feel about the spirits of the dead? Is a ghost just a bogey? Try Yeats's *All Souls' Night*.

The Straw (p. 111) is characteristic of Graves's later love poetry 'The wild valley streaked with torrents' evokes in a few words the landscape that can be seen from the poet's house in Majorca.

THOM GUNN, b. 1929

An Englishman, educated at Cambridge, Thom Gunn has for some years made his home in California, and *On the Move* (p. 52) shows him at grips with a social phenomenon (the 'Wild Ones' or *blousons noirs*) which, originating there, has since become familiar in every Western country. The problem—what drives them so endlessly and so fast?—has been discussed by sociologists, educationalists, policemen, psychologists, etc.; Gunn approaches it as a poet, and his imaginative sympathy seems to me to outweigh, in these few lines, most of the other contributions. Did someone say that poetry does not concern itself with everyday life?

Neither *St Martin and the Beggar* (p. 122) nor the beautiful lyric *Jesus and his Mother* (p. 92) call for comment; here again Thom Gunn is bringing the distant and the mysterious down to everyday terms—understanding a thing simply by imagining it.

THOMAS HARDY, 1840–1928

Hardy, an old-fashioned and rustic person, would have been surprised to see himself in an anthology of 'modern' poetry, yet one includes him as naturally as one includes Hopkins. Both were alike in banishing from their poetry everything merely 'literary', merely copied out of books and not heard on the lips of living men. Hardy began as a poet, turned to novel-writing when he found that his poetry could not get a hearing (again one thinks of Hopkins), and finally returned to poetry when his novels had won him a reputation and smoothed the path to publication. The language of his poetry, a heightened and exalted version of the language of his novels, has a gnarled and rustic quality; his poems seem like roots dug up from the Wessex clay. Together, Hopkins and Hardy form a bridge between the professional expertness of the Tennyson-to-Swin-burne era, and the modern cosmopolitanism of the Pound-Eliot *nouvelle vague*.

Drummer Hodge (p. 164) shares with the much later *Transformations* (p. 81) the typically Hardyesque sense of 'dust to dust'. Drummer Hodge typifies the English country boys who were killed in the Boer War; Rupert Brooke found the idea worth taking over for his much-quoted sonnet written in 1914, *The Soldier*. I can see why Brooke's poem should have been popular, but Hardy's seems to me much the better: do you agree?

To an Unborn Pauper Child (p. 85), another early poem, illustrates that pessimism of Hardy's which G. K. Chesterton had in mind when he savagely described Hardy as 'the village atheist brooding and blaspheming over the village idiot'. Which do you prefer, this poem or Louis MacNeice's *Prayer before Birth* (p. 84)?

Afterwards (p. 174) seems to me Hardy's best, and one of the great English poems: lofty in conception, calm and strong in execution. Those who want to understand the concept of 'form' in poetry might find it worth asking why the short lines and close-set rhymes of, say, *Transformations* seem exactly right for what the poem is saying, while the long, sweeping rhythms and widely spaced rhymes of *Afterwards* also seem exactly right.

Or why, for that matter, *The Voice* (p. 106) makes use of a rhythmical movement very rare in modern poetry, the 'dactyl' (one heavy beat followed by two light ones). Is it for the hesitant, faltering effect of the rhymes 'call to me—all to me', etc., intensifying the pathos? Do you feel that 'wistless-ness', so obviously introduced as a last-ditch rhyme for 'listlessness', is a serious blemish on the poem? Could any other poet get away with such an apparently clumsy word?

GEOFFREY HILL, b. 1932

A strong and original poet whose work seems built to last, Geoffrey Hill first began publishing poetry as an Oxford undergraduate, now teaches at Leeds University.

Those interested in literary 'influences' will see in *Requiem for the Plantagenet Kings* (p. 166) an example of how a poet can learn from Hopkins's sonnets without being in any sense an imitator. Hopkins showed that this kind of dense, craggy sonnet was possible; Hill writes it in his own idiom.

GERARD MANLEY HOPKINS, 1844–1889

Hopkins, a Jesuit priest whose Order employed him first in general parish work and latterly as Professor of Classics at University College, Dublin, was one of the greatest of the English poets; his achievement was, in view of the utter isolation in which he worked, almost incredible. His position is, roughly, outlined in the Introduction (p. 22); the nature of his achievement only emerges clearly from a close look at the poems themselves, particularly if one reads them in their true contemporary setting, beside Swinburne, William Morris, the later Browning and Tennyson. Hopkins belongs with the modern poets because he anticipated their discoveries about the poetic use of language; but, whereas they had (and have) support from one another and from modern criticism, Hopkins worked in loneliness and silence, while the quality of the 'criticism' he could expect if he showed his poems to the literary men of that time is sufficiently indicated by a glance at THE LETTERS OF GERARD MANLEY HOPKINS AND ROBERT BRIDGES (Oxford University Press, 1935), a great tragi-comic book. The essential material for an intelligent study of Hopkins is contained in the excellent selection from his verse and prose made by W. H. Gardner for Penguin Books (THE PENGUIN POETS, D 15).

The Candle Indoors (p. 39). A typical Hopkinsian poem in praise of the beauty of everyday things and gratitude to God. The light of the candle is so 'blissful' that he wishes he could see the cottager, a man or woman, who carries on some household task by its light, so as to complete the scene with a human presence that could express thanks to God. The phrase 'to-fro tender trambeams truckle at the eye' has been frequently cited for derision by those who find Hopkins obscure and eccentric; actually it can be justified. Tram-lines in a wet city street at night (a commoner sight to Hopkins than to us) shine with long yellow lines of light, very similar to those we see if we look at a candle-flame through lowered eyelashes, and just as 'tender'. A truckle-bed ran on castors so as to be pushed under an ordinary bed, hence to 'truckle to' someone means to give in to him, to accept him as the more important; the beams move gently—as it were, deferentially—to and from the eye, like something running on tram-lines, or like a truckle-bed.

Felix Randal (p. 163) is, like *The Candle Indoors*, a sonnet in strict form, but in this case Hopkins has lengthened the line to a basic six feet instead of five, to give himself more room for the sweeping, alliterative roll of his characteristic verse movement, which he himself called 'sprung rhythm'. The priest muses on the death of one of his flock. Felix Randal is dead, and the priest's duty all ended. Yet the relationship that came into being during those months of sickness cannot be cancelled; it stays in the priest's life as a permanent thing. Without any hint of pride, in fact with a delicate and touching humility, he thinks better of himself because he was able to be of some help. The give-and-take between the dying man and his comforter is beautifully suggested in the echoing 'touch—tears—tears—touched' of lines 10 and 11.

The Windhover (p. 73) is one of the most commented-on poems in English, and it is impossible to offer an interpretation of it without being at once contradicted by someone or other. Basically, however, its content is quite simple. One of Hopkins's recurrent themes is the adoration of God through His handi-work in Nature. The falcon is the 'dauphin' of the 'kingdom of daylight', i.e. a favoured child though not the king. That king, Christ, is addressed by the poet as 'my chevalier'; medieval and heraldic imagery crops up all through the poem, as in *minion, wimpling, plume, buckle,* etc. No wonder such a beautiful creature as a falcon should inspire us with love of the Creator, when even such humdrum things as a furrow newly turned by the plough, or an almost-burnt coal in the fire, can suddenly reveal—they too!—astonishing beauty. That is, broadly, the surface move-ment of the poem, but there is much more for the attentive reader. The closing lines, for instance, with their insistence on cutting and wounding ('gall themselves, and gash') and perhaps on dullness and routine ('sheer plod'—though 'sheer' of course is an intentional pun) contain the suggestion that beauty is bought with suffering.

No Worst, there is None (p. 174) is one of the so-called 'terrible sonnets' in which Hopkins explores the suffering which so often invades the tranquillity of the cloistered life. Though he has renounced the world and given his life to God, he often feels as far away as ever from any true one-ness with God. Such a poem as this very frankly expresses the despair which can invade the soul and which Christians regard as a sin; 'all life death does end' sounds more like an atheist's consolation than a priest's, and it is typical of Hopkins that he does not attempt to soften this mood.

Binsey Poplars (p. 78) laments the beginning of that destruction of the beauty of Oxford's rural outskirts which has gone on faster and faster until our own time, when the job has been completed. The axe-strokes 'unselve' the rural scene, i.e. rob it of that essential individuality which is the core of all being. Hopkins was a follower of the theologian Duns Scotus, rather than of St Thomas Aquinas as would have been more usual in a Jesuit; Scotus lays great emphasis on the selfhood or final individual quality of a person or thing, which he called its *haecceitas* (thisness). Hopkins's doctrine of the 'inscape', with which there is no need to concern ourselves here, derives in part from his assent to this view.

The Sea and the Skylark (p. 73) voices Hopkins's pessimism about what man is doing to the world and himself, coupled with his unshakeable joy in the world as it issued from the hand of the Creator. In his letters to friends, his condemnation of 'our sordid turbid time' is very downright. Lines 4 to 8 show that, in spite of the example of Shelley, it *is* possible to write about a skylark in such a way as to convey what kind of sound it makes and why we like listening to it.

TED HUGHES, b. 1930

Born in Yorkshire, educated at Cambridge, Ted Hughes has worked at a number of jobs, including a spell of university teaching in America; but his preference seems to be for a rural, open-air life, and he is at present farming in Devon. His poems, with their strong, unsentimental flavour and their loving observation of all forms of life, are very much a countryman's.

He is represented here not by any of his poems about animals (which are numerous and excellent), but by two poems which show his feeling for the dark, instinctual side of life. *Witches* (p. 103) offers a view of the nature of witchcraft that can certainly not be brushed aside by scientific enlightenment. *Gog* (p. 127) refers to the biblical prophecy (Ezekiel, chapter xxviii) of a hostile power that will arise in the world immediately before the Last Judgment, and inflict untold destruction.

ELIZABETH JENNINGS, b. 1926

A still, meditative poet, Miss Jennings has written a book about the relationship between poetry and mystical experience (EVERY CHANGING SHAPE, 1961), as well as a considerable body of verse. Her work is tinged by her Roman Catholicism, though not in any obvious, surface way, and one feels that she aims at a translucent poetry in which the words are like polished panes of glass through which light and colour shine without adulteration.

SIDNEY KEYES, 1922–1943

One of the most original new poets of the war-time period with its movement away from the topicality and the argumentation of the 'thirties, Sidney Keyes was killed in action. *War Poet* (p. 139) poignantly expresses his personal situation.

CAROLYN KIZER, b. 1925 (U.S.A.)

Born in Spokane, Carolyn Kizer travelled widely before settling in Seattle, her present home. She represented the Institute of Pacific Relations at international conferences in England and Japan, was a Fellow of the Chinese Government in Comparative Literature at Columbia University, New York, and spent some months in China just before the Nationalist Government fell. She has three children.

A Muse of Water (p. 101) is a poem about being a woman, and more particularly a woman with a creative talent. (The Muses are female, and a woman poet could be called a Muse, but so, too, could any woman who was loved by a man and helped him to find his creative powers.) The poem turns on images of water; the woman's life is typified by the traditional symbol of fluidity whether it is at the kitchen tap or the royal barge. A child, before birth, floats in the amniotic fluid in its mother's body, and afterwards she suckles it; how can this liquid, flowing existence add upto Life, let alone to Art? The poem tells us how. It is very much 'what oft was thought but ne'er so well expressed'; I never remember seeing a poem on this subject before, yet it organizes into one whole a great many thoughts that everyone has had.

STANLEY KUNITZ, b. 1905 (U.S.A.)

Educated at Harvard, Stanley Kunitz has earned a living by various teaching posts and by editing books of reference, notably TWENTIETH CENTURY AUTHORS. He now lives in New York and conducts the Poetry Workshop at the Poetry Center, an institution of which there is no English equivalent.

Benediction (p. 66) and *The War against the Trees* (p. 79) are good examples of Stanley Kunitz's open, lyrical style, and need no comment. *Foreign Affairs* (p. 116) is worth close attention as an example of the way a poet can sustain one metaphor throughout an entire poem, talking about two things at once and never saying anything that does not apply with equal force to both. Professor Wilson Knight has said that a typical Shakespeare play is 'an extended metaphor'. Yes, and not only a Shakespeare play.

PHILIP LARKIN, b. 1922

A Midlander (his father was City Treasurer of Coventry), Philip Larkin was educated at Oxford and now works as a university librarian. His poetry is quiet, reflective, with beautifully precise statements and delicate rhythms, yet surprisingly capable, at moments, of a robust irony and an almost farcical sense of fun; he is one of the few poets who can be genuinely funny without ceasing to write what is recognizably poetry. Most of his work, however, is gently melancholy, particularly when he writes of the effect of time on people and their relationships. As he puts it in one of his poems,

> Truly, though our element is time,
> We are not suited to the long perspectives
> Open at each instant of our lives.

I Remember, I Remember (p. 95) shows Larkin in his sardonic vein; you probably recall the touching little poem by Hood from which the title is taken. One's actual memories of boyhood, Larkin seems to be saying, are much more complicated and, so often, much more negative; and he goes on to poke fun at the whole Technicolor myth of growing up as sentimental writers have presented it, plus the memoirs of ageing men of genius, whose childhood recollections (suitably arranged) always include moments of piercing imaginative vision (being spoken to by an old hat).

Church Going (p. 168) starts in a similar vein of dry humour, but mounts up to an impassioned statement on a very important theme—the thoughts of a man who values the Church although he no longer believes in the religion it enshrines, and is trying to get at his real reasons for valuing it. This poem will repay careful pondering. What, for instance, is the exact process whereby 'our compulsions meet' and are 'robed as destinies'? What is the 'ghostly silt', now 'dispersed'?

ROBERT LOWELL, b. 1917 (U.S.A.)

Born in Boston, Robert Lowell was educated at Harvard, and subsequently studied with John Crowe Ransom at Kenyon College in Ohio. His poetry has attracted much attention both in America and in England; his second volume, published in 1946, won the Pulitzer Prize and since then he has received various prizes, fellowships and awards; he has also served as Poetry Consultant to the Library of Congress.

A member of an historic Boston family, Robert Lowell has a natural interest in the past, in ancestry, tradition and in that history which, in New England, makes itself so strongly felt. In

LIFE STUDIES (1959) he has given us what amounts to an autobiography in a sequence of poems, dealing with his childhood,
memories of various members of his family and vignettes of his
life as an adult.

The Quaker Graveyard in Nantucket (p. 152) was occasioned by the
death by drowning of the poet's cousin during the Second World
War. Nantucket, on the stormy coast of New England, is the
port of departure for the desperate whale-hunt described in
Melville's MOBY DICK; it is also the site of a cemetery where
lie the bones of peace-loving Quakers, men and women who
have refused strife and violence and built their lives on quiet-
ness. This paradox, especially striking to a New England poet,
lies at the centre of the poem.

This poem is difficult, but to elucidate it completely would
need a long essay, and the clues are there for the alert reader;
the difficulty comes from the density with which meaning is
packed down on meaning. English readers will realize that
Madaket and 'Sconset (i.e. Siasconset) are coastal places in
Nantucket; Woods Hole is a town on the south-western
end, and Martha's Vineyard an island, south of Cape Cod.
Ahab (l.15) is the maniacal whaler-captain in MOBY DICK.
In Section IV the references are biblical and religious. The
chapel of Our Lady in Walsingham Priory, Norfolk, was a
famous shrine until its destruction by Henry VIII; partly
restored in 1921, it was evidently visited by Warren Winslow. Shiloah or Shiloh was where the Israelites set up the
Tabernacle and the Ark of the Covenant after their expulsion
from Jerusalem; Sion, by contrast, was the hill in Jerusalem
where the Temple stood. The sailor 'whistled Sion' when he got
to Walsingham because he felt he had come home, to a permanent spiritual resting-place. *Non est species, neque decor* means
'There is no form nor comeliness'.

Like all great elegies, from Milton's *Lycidas* through Shelley's
Adonais and Tennyson's *In Memoriam* to Whitman's *When Lilac*

Last in the Dooryard Bloomed, this poem begins with the death of one individual person and builds up to include the poet himself, his world and his ultimate values and motives: necessarily, for no other tribute is complete enough to honour the dead man.

NORMAN MacCAIG, b. 1910

While not going to the length of rejecting the English language altogether and writing in some more or less artificial form of 'Scots', Norman MacCaig writes poetry that is Scottish through and through, in its blend of the concrete and earthy with the abstract and speculative; Louis MacNeice has called it 'physical metaphysical'.

Laggandoan, Harris (p. 77) is a pure celebration of the beauty of a Hebridean landscape, and would make a very interesting comparison with a classic English 'nature poem' such as Housman's *'Tis time, I think, by Wenlock town.*

LOUIS MacNEICE, 1907–1963

Like most of the poets who began publishing in the early 'thirties, Louis MacNeice shows signs of the all-pervading influence of Auden, but he was from the beginning a poet who knew his own mind. An Ulsterman, son of a bishop, classical scholar, he took a cool, shrewd, disenchanted look at the scene; free from the rather undergraduate enthusiasms of those left-wing days, and yet not reactionary or unfeeling, he distilled poetry out of a certain irony, sad on top but gay and fizzing underneath. His use of language and his rhythms are always personal—a MacNeice poem can be recognized anywhere—and the spare elegance of his verse recalls, in its own very individual way, the work of other classically trained poets like Housman and Bridges. In the normality and sanity of its attitudes MacNeice's poetry speaks for the 'plain man', or rather for what the plain man would be if he were to become shrewder, more sensitive, more intelligent, without ceasing to be direct and straightforward.

MacNeice's COLLECTED POEMS came out in 1949, but he wrote about as much again before his death in 1963. He worked for the B.B.C., as producer and writer, for some twenty years, and has shown a special interest in the radio play, e.g. CHRISTOPHER COLUMBUS (1944) and THE DARK TOWER (1947). He also memorably translated THE AGAMEMNON of Aeschylus and Goethe's FAUST, and wrote a stage play, OUT OF THE PICTURE (1937).

An Eclogue for Christmas (p. 44) was the show-piece of MacNeice's first mature volume, POEMS (1935). The word 'eclogue', originally applied to Virgil's ten pastoral poems, came during the Renaissance to apply to rustic dialogues, and finally any dialogues, in verse; this one is between a townsman and a countryman. England of the mid-'thirties is here seen from the point of view of a discontent no less real than Auden's, but less self-consciously dramatized and more matter-of-fact. 'The good things which in the end turn to poison and pus' (p. 47) are the middle-class trappings of comfort and security, like the 'plate-glass windows of the Sport Hotel' or the 'efficient band' which both tourist and farmer hear on the radio (p. 41).

Brother Fire (p. 159) is, of course, a war poem. It gets very close to the inner truth of the civilian's feelings under bombardment; there is a wish to destroy in every human being, and the sight of smashed and burning buildings can unleash a terrifying joy as well as pity and fear. Once again MacNeice has shown the complexity and depth of everyday, 'normal' emotions. Likewise the conscript and the unborn child are average human beings, caught in the universal human situation which the poet makes it his business to explore.

E. H. W. MEYERSTEIN, 1889–1952

Meyerstein was a prolific, uneven poet, whose huge output has been creamed by Maurice Wollman in SOME POEMS BY E. H. W. MEYERSTEIN (1959). Recluse, scholar, eccentric, he hated the modern world and yet merits inclusion in an anthology of 'modern' poetry because the strange, tortured angularity of his vision represents a break with the past as complete as anyone's. Like T. S. Eliot (whom he bitterly criticized), Meyerstein found more poetic nutriment in the seventeenth century than in anything more recent. For a portrait of this extraordinary man, see his posthumous OF MY EARLY LIFE, edited by Rowland Watson (1957) and John Wain, SPRIGHTLY RUNNING (1962), pp. 103–36.

EDWIN MUIR, 1887–1958

A Scottish poet, whose work was entirely individual in its combination of a quiet, rather staid language with a visionary content, Muir has devotees to whom his poetry is some of the most important written in our century. I do not share this view myself, yet I can sympathize with it; a quiet pool may contain more interesting life than a raging torrent, and Muir's COLLECTED POEMS 1921–51 (1952) is full of fine things, especially for the more thoughtful reader. He was also an excellent critic of literature and ideas, e.g. in THE STRUCTURE OF THE NOVEL (1928), SCOTT AND SCOTLAND (1936), THE SCOTS AND THEIR COUNTRY (1936) and ESSAYS ON LITERATURE AND SOCIETY (1949).

The Animals (p. 71) shows Muir the visionary poet, looking at the whole of creation from a standpoint in eternity.

The Castle (p. 53) represents another typical kind of Muir poem, the short symbolic fable which can be reduced to a prose 'meaning' readily enough—but goes on reverberating in the reader's mind in a way that makes any paraphrase seem finally unsatisfactory.

WILFRED OWEN, 1893–1918

Only four of Owen's poems were published in his lifetime. Siegfried Sassoon, a brother officer whose poetry did much to challenge Owen into writing, edited a posthumous collection in 1920, from which it was immediately obvious that the First World War had robbed England of a major poet—a poet whose surviving work, appropriately enough, concerns itself largely with a passionate attack on the folly and cruelty of war. Owen, who served in the Artists' Rifles from the outbreak of war, was invalided out in 1917, but recovered in time to return to France, where he saw further fighting, was awarded the M.C. and died in battle only a week before the Armistice.

Of all the voices that have been raised against war, Owen's is the loftiest and the most poignant. And from the purely literary point of view, he deserves his place in an anthology of 'modern' poetry, for his terse, packed style and his rapid half-rhymes look forward to much in the poetic era of which he would, surely, have been one of the giants. *Strange Meeting* (p. 139) shows these qualities. It is usually called an unfinished poem, because it breaks off; but it is difficult to see how it could have gone any further.

SYLVIA PLATH, 1932–1963 (U.S.A.)

A native of Boston, Sylvia Plath was educated at Smith College, Mass., and Newnham College, Cambridge. After her marriage to Ted Hughes, she settled in England. Her death in 1963 was widely felt as a grievous loss to poetry.

Sylvia Plath's is a very feminine poetry, with its delicacy of perception and its care for things that need to be cherished and nurtured. *Mushrooms* (p. 68) makes an interesting comparison with Roethke's *The Small* (p. 67), as a masculine and feminine treatment of much the same theme. *Morning Song* (p. 91) is also a completely feminine poem; on such a theme, it could hardly fail to be; but what, after all, is meant by 'masculine' or 'feminine' as applied to poetry? How can the terms be usefully applied? Does Sylvia Plath's verse strike you as more essentially feminine than that of Christich Rossetti or Elizabeth Barrett Browning? Or the other women contributors to this book? If Emily Dickinson and Edith Sitwell are both 'feminine' poets, are we trying to make the word mean too much? For that matter, is Jane Austen really more feminine than, say, Dickens?

EZRA POUND, b. 1885 (U.S.A.)

Born at Hailey, Idaho, Ezra Pound first crossed the Atlantic in 1901, when he went to Spain on a grant from the University of Pennsylvania. He was sent to undertake literary research, and in a sense literary research in its widest form—investigation of the nature of civilization and how it can be aided by good writing—is what he has been doing ever since. After a brief spell as a college teacher in America, Pound returned to Europe again and lived there—in London, in Paris and, after 1924, in Italy—until 1945. In that year he was arrested by the U.S. military authorities and taken back to America on a charge of treason. The charge was not denied, for Pound had been making pro-Italian (and therefore, by implication, pro-German) broadcasts over Rome radio for some years; but a panel of doctors found him unfit to plead and 'in need of care in a mental hospital'. He was accordingly confined in St Elizabeth's Hospital, Washington D.C., until 1959, when he was released and went to Italy to live with his daughter and her husband.

People who dislike Pound have therefore had plenty of

opportunity to describe him as a traitor (during the war) and a madman (since his commitment to hospital). The actual facts of the case are more delicate. Pound has given his life to the struggle to improve the lot of mankind; in his view, art is one of the major instruments for doing this; economics is another. He has always been opposed to a financial system which rests on investment and interest-rates (or, to give it its old and more forthright name, usury), and when Mussolini seized power in Italy, Pound was not without hope of converting Il Duce to his own brand of reformist economics and thus beginning a new period of social justice in which war and famine would be impossible.

These ideas may have been deluded, though I would advise anyone not to jump to that conclusion before finding out in detail what they are; all I have space for here is to point out that Pound used the Italian radio to put over ideas which he had been advocating for ten years and which he genuinely believed would benefit the world. Of course, when America went to war against Italy it immediately became treasonable for Pound to express these views over the air, but in this connection it is worth quoting two sentences from the medical report which his doctors submitted at the time of the trial:

At the present time, he exhibits extremely poor judgment as to his situation. He insists that his broadcasts were not treasonable but that all of his radio activities have stemmed from his self-appointed mission to 'save the Constitution'.

The 'Constitution' that Pound saw himself as trying to 'save' is the American Constitution, especially as it derives from Thomas Jefferson, one of the heroes of his epic poem THE CANTOS. In all this it will at least be conceded that Pound, even if technically he did find himself in the position of 'giving aid and comfort to the enemy', never acted like the common-or-garden renegade who changes sides because he thinks that the enemy is going to win, or because he has a grudge against his own country.

'Δώρια' (p. 173; more usually, Δώρεια) means gifts, and especially generous gifts, bounty. The poem captures the terse yet lyrical note of the poems in the Greek Anthology. To see in more detail what this amounts to, consult Dudley Fitts's FROM THE GREEK ANTHOLOGY (1957), a series of free translations from this great source-book of Greek lyric poetry, much influenced by Pound: or, for an earlier version free from Pound's influence, J. W. Mackail's SELECT EPIGRAMS FROM THE GREEK ANTHOLOGY (1911). It is all part of Pound's effort to re-create, in a modern vein, the essence of what he finds valuable in past cultures: in other words, to 'Make It New'. Likewise in *Homage to Sextus Propertius* (p. 60) Pound takes the ironic, savage, tender, sophisticated elegies of the Roman poet and produces something between a translation and an adaptation. The idea of such writing is not new; in the eighteenth century such poems were known as 'Imitations', and were a recognized genre. Dr Johnson's *Vanity of Human Wishes* is an 'imitation' of Juvenal's Tenth Satire. Ezra Pound is the greatest modern exponent of the 'Imitation', whether the poetry he is re-creating is Greek, Latin, Chinese, Provençal or Elizabethan English. In *Dance Figure* (p. 107) the original seems to be not poetry, in the ordinary sense, at all, but the New Testament (for subject-matter) and the Old Testament (for the rhythms). The one thing common to all Pound's hundreds of 'Imitations' is his unerring sense of how to blend the singing with the speaking voice, the lyrical with the matter-of-fact. To appreciate this is far more important than to pick up every one of Pound's cosmopolitan and multilingual fragments. Thus, for example, to sort out the precise reason why Pound attributes *Taking Leave of a Friend* (p. 49) to 'Rihaku' is interesting if you happen to be interested in that kind of thing; the original is by the classical Chinese poet Li Po, of whose name Rihaku is the Japanese form; Pound calls him Rihaku because he is following the version of the American scholar Ernest Fenellosa, who had (for various complicated reasons) transliterated a number of Chinese poems into the Japanese written form before putting them into English. The main interest of Pound's Chinese 'Imitations' lies not in such details, revealing as they often are, but in the fact that he has opened a window into the world of classical Chinese poetry, which the rest of us can look through.

Canto XLV (p. 54) shows Pound in didactic vein, reminding us that he is a great 'teaching' poet; the Cantos, on which he has been engaged for thirty-odd years, cannot be summarized here (an excellent short account of their main drift will be found in G. S. Fraser's EZRA POUND, 1960), but one of the main themes running all through the poem is Pound's hatred of usury, here called by its Latin name, doubtless to fit in better with the classical-cum-renaissance atmosphere of this magnificent denunciation. Pound has always insisted that the human race must have enduring masterpieces, handed down and treasured from generation to generation, if its life is to be anything more than a random succession of incidents; usury, and the profit motive generally, produces goods for quick sale, with no thought of permanence, and this is its real 'sin against nature'.

JOHN CROWE RANSOM, b. 1888 (U.S.A.)

Though he has lived for a good many years in Ohio, John Crowe Ransom is a Southerner who has spent most of his life in Tennessee. His poetry is elegant, wry and, in a subdued but quite unrepentant fashion, courtly.

Old Man playing with Children (p. 129) makes an interesting comparison with Yeats's *Prayer for Old Age* (p. 175).

THEODORE ROETHKE, 1908–1963 (U.S.A.)

A middle Westerner, Theodore Roethke lived a wandering and adventurous life, and held down a variety of jobs ranging from professional tennis coach through pickle-factory worker to university teacher. He published his first volume of poems in 1941, but only came into his full reputation with his book WORDS FOR THE WIND in 1957.

Roethke's poems celebrate the instinctual life and the things that lie on the edge of consciousness. *The Small* (p. 67) and *Snake* (p. 74) are typical of his meditations on the half-glimpsed life that is all about us and of which we never succeed in forming a clear picture. *Words for the Wind* (p. 112) seems to me one of the great love poems of our time; the debt to Yeats is obvious, and there is an evident kinship with Dylan Thomas, another poet who held that 'Those who embrace, believe', and yet lines like 'the oyster's weeping foot' and 'she moves when time is shy' are pure Roethke. He has a kaleidoscopic gift which enables his work to remind one of many other poets and yet always remain itself.

STEPHEN SPENDER, b. 1909

Born into a well-known family in London (his uncle, J. A. Spender, was an influential journalist, and his father stood for Parliament), Stephen Spender was educated at Oxford and during his student years and afterwards spent much time in Germany; he is partly German on his mother's side. His contact with W. H. Auden at Oxford, and Christopher Isherwood in Germany, are described in his autobiography WORLD WITHIN WORLD (1951). Like all the 'Auden group', but in a characteristically passionate and idealistic way, Spender was drawn to left-wing politics during the 'thirties. In 1937 he spent several months in Spain; back in England, he served as a fireman during the war and also helped Cyril Connolly to edit the magazine HORIZON. Since 1953 he has been co-editor of the Anglo-American magazine ENCOUNTER.

Spender's poetry was from the start more rhapsodic than that of Auden or MacNeice, and has been attacked for sentimentality, verbal imprecision and a host of other faults. But at its best it is moving and memorable; what appears in the weaker poems as *naiveté* emerges, in the stronger ones, as an extraordinary transparency, a lack of evasive techniques, which carries him straight to the heart of the subject. The poems I have chosen for this book do not seem to require any individual comment.

WALLACE STEVENS, 1879–1955 (U.S.A.)

Stevens, a giant among modern poets, is for the most part too difficult for an anthology of this kind, but he could not be left out altogether; he has a spare, hypnotic music all his own, and any reader of poetry ought to try his colossal COLLECTED POEMS (1955).

Dry Loaf (p. 39), which I take to be a meditation, half poetic and half musical, on the statement contained in its first two lines, is a good example of the delicate balance of sight and sound in Stevens's poetry.

DOUGLAS STEWART, b. 1913

Australia, like every English-speaking country, is rich in poets; it is impossible to give anything like a fair representation of them here, so I abandoned any attempt to pick out a 'typical' modern Australian poem and fell back on a personal favourite of mine, Douglas Stewart's *The Silkworms* (p. 75). Actually this poet was born in New Zealand, but since settling in Australia in 1938 he has concerned himself largely with Australian themes and settings. As poet, critic, short-story writer and literary editor of THE BULLETIN, he has made his influence widely felt in Australian letters.

Do you read *The Silkworms* completely 'straight', as a poem about a certain kind of insect? Or do the symbolic overtones guide your thoughts away from insects and towards situations inherent in all life? Is this a 'symbolic' poem? Or is every poem symbolic? Some people refuse to spend time over any poem that does not at once yield up its full meaning. Would they enjoy this poem?

ALLEN TATE, b. 1899 (U.S.A.)

Like John Crowe Ransom, with whom he has often been associated in the public literary mind, Allen Tate is a Southerner (born in Kentucky), who has earned his living mainly as a university professor. His poetry has been recognized as important since his first volume appeared in 1928; as a critic he matured more slowly, but his REACTIONARY ESSAYS (1936) and REASON IN MADNESS (1941) were at once seen to be work of classic importance. Tate has also written a famous novel, THE FATHERS (1938), and made contributions to American history with his studies of Stonewall Jackson and Jefferson Davis. He was converted to Roman Catholicism in 1950.

Ode to the Confederate Dead (p. 147) is an elaborate and complex poem, written in a language which is both rhetorical, reaching out for large effects, and intellectual, refusing simplifications. The soldiers who died fighting for the confederate (i.e. Southern) cause in the American Civil War have been honoured by Southerners with platitudes enough; here is one Southerner who will write about them without using any of the *clichés*, though he is willing enough to pay his homage at the accustomed time (to 'bow his head with a commemorial woe').

The best way to the heart of this difficult but magnificent poem is to read it over and over again and let it work its magic, before we strive too impatiently for analysis. Its form is worth careful examination. Dante, in his critical treatise DE VUL-GARI ELOQUENTIA, said that the highest form of vernacular poetry was the *canzone* of tragic style dealing with a lofty subject. This is such a *canzone*. The form may be described as a poem in stanzas of length to be determined by the poet, usually up to twenty lines or so, and with an elaborate rhyme-scheme also decided on by the poet. Once the stanza is devised, it has to be strictly observed, and the form also requires a certain number of six-syllable lines inserted among the ten-syllable (in Italian, eleven-syllable) lines that make up the staple of the poem. Tate has treated the form with a certain freedom, but then so did Milton in *Lycidas*.

Those who do not read Italian can study a perfectly regular *canzone* in Edmund Spenser's *Prothalamion*.

DYLAN THOMAS, 1914–1953

The son of a Swansea schoolmaster, Dylan Thomas worked briefly, after leaving school, as a cub reporter on a local news-paper. He then went to London, where he worked at a variety of literary jobs, managing, however, to concentrate on his poetry, which gained an immediate hearing on the publication of 18 POEMS in 1934. The B.B.C. became increasingly interested in Thomas's gifts as a verse-speaker, and (particularly after the coming of the Third Programme in 1946) he broadcast fre-quently, and also travelled the country giving public readings. Thomas was the first poet to enter whole-heartedly the new (or restored ancient) relationship with the public made possible by broadcasting and sound-recording; it suited his bardic style of delivery, and created an audience for his public appearances. Towards the end of his life the whole highly organized business of public appearances began, as it did in the comparable case of Dickens, to assume the proportions of an avalanche (see J. M. Brinnin, DYLAN THOMAS IN AMERICA), and there can be no doubt that the strain led directly to that combination of physical exhaustion and alcoholism which resulted in his premature death. For an account of his place in the development of twentieth-century poetry, see the Introduction.

The force that through the green fuse drives the flower (p. 94) and *Light breaks where no sun shines* (p. 104) are both from Thomas's first volume, 18 POEMS, published when he was twenty. They are poems of adolescence, full of wildness, longing and urgent physical sensation. A rigorous critic could object to almost all these early poems, and certainly to the two included here, that they deal in large phrases and that sometimes the phrases are too large for the meanings: the poet is not quite able to fill his reverberating lines with sufficient matter; one recalls Keats's advice to Shelley: 'Curb your magnanimity and load every rift with ore'. This admitted, they still seem to me fine and important poems, expressing a passionate sense of union with all created nature. It is interesting to compare these two poems with the 'Lucy' poems of Wordsworth—the same pantheistic attitude, but a very different poetic idiom.

In the middle and later 'thirties Thomas's poetry became clotted and often impenetrably obscure, before opening out to the much more accessible manner of DEATHS AND ENTRANCES, of which *Poem in October* (p. 98) is a splendid example. *In my Craft or Sullen Art* (p. 60), *The Hunchback in the Park* (p. 120) and *Among those killed in the dawn raid was a man aged a hundred* (p. 137) are all equally open, but Thomas's great elegy *A Refusal to Mourn the Death, by Fire, of a Child in London* (p. 160) is written with something of the density of his earlier poems. It is not difficult to paraphrase, provided we begin by noting that the first sentence lasts for thirteen lines, so that we do not reach a full stop until (properly enough) the word *death*; also, the main verb of that first sentence, *shall*, does not occur until half-way through the second stanza. The poet says that he will never mourn for the child until the darkness ushers out the last light and brings all things to an end—

whether for him personally, at his death, or more broadly at the end of the world, does not greatly matter within the framework of the poem. Since to be born is to emerge from darkness into light, the darkness is described in the opening lines as 'mankind making' and 'bird beast and flower fathering'; since we are all equal, and all powerless, in darkness—i.e. when dead, not yet born, or asleep—the darkness is also all humbling: the poet at his death will be merged with the basic material of the world, and the words 'Zion' and 'synagogue', along with the biblical and liturgical echoes found consistently throughout the poem ('the stations of the breath', for example, recalls the Stations of the Cross in the Roman Catholic mass), indicate that this merging, both as it will happen to the poet, and as it has already happened to the child, is seen as holy. The last stanza contains a few verbal puzzles, but the difficulty is only on the surface: the 'long friends' are the grains of London earth; they are beyond age, because it is impossible to estimate the age of a grain of sand, and this makes them long (i.e. long-standing, permanent) friends to the child—but the word 'long' also refers back to 'robed', and brings into the mind the picture of the girl dressed in a ceremonial shroud. The word 'grain' also suggests resurrection and a new life.

These hints should help in getting at the poem's 'prose meaning'; but getting a grasp of this is only the first step towards appreciating the poem. Thomas was a great poetic musician, and he has orchestrated this poem, not only by means of its imagery, but with every device of harmony. All textbooks tell us that poets use alliteration, but one cannot learn from a textbook to write lines like

Deep with the first dead lies London's daughter.

The same textbooks tell us that poets use assonance, but it takes a poet to write

The grains beyond age, the dark veins of her mother.

Do not go gentle into that good night (p. 172), one of the last poems Thomas wrote, shows among other things how attentively he had read his Yeats, whose influence can also be seen in *In my Craft or Sullen Art*—though in both cases it is finely assimilated to Thomas's personal music. The vilanelle, after centuries of almost complete neglect, had recently been revived by William Empson (see *Missing Dates*, p. 171), and Thomas, who was a friend of Empson's, may have been following his example here. This poem has been admirably set to music by Elizabeth Lutyens.

R. S. THOMAS, b. 1913

Though a Welshman, R. S. Thomas was not brought up in a bi-lingual tradition, and he learnt Welsh in order to establish a closer contact between himself and the rural people about whose lives he so often writes in his poetry. After graduating from University College, Bangor, he attended Llandaff Theological College and was ordained in 1936. He is now Vicar of Eglwys Fach, Cardiganshire.

TERENCE TILLER, b. 1915

Nothing shows the indifference of our age to poetry more than the comparative neglect of a fine poet like Terence Tiller. His is a pure poetic voice: what he offers is poetry and not something else disguising itself as poetry. It does not draw attention to itself by loudness or surface novelty; nor does it nudge the reader, but waits for him to make his own discoveries.

Poems For One Person (p. 109) appeared in the war-time anthology PERSONAL LANDSCAPE when the poet was serving in the Middle East, and indicated Tiller's distance both from the political poetry of the Auden years and the wilder lyricism of the 1940's. In such poems as these, his vision and his use of language are closer to those of John Donne than to any contemporary poet; come to them freshly after *A Nocturnal Upon St Lucy's Day* or *A Fever*, and much of their strangeness vanishes.

Street Performers, 1851 (p. 128) seems at first glance to be an unambitious poem, a water-colour of mid-Victorian London inspired by a few lines from Mayhew's great survey. Yet on attentive reading we find that the whole of that London is captured in the poem, its desperation and hunger as well as its surface variety and fun.

fantoccini: Italian puppets

CONSTANTINE TRYPANIS, b. 1909

Born on the island of Chios in the Aegean, Constantine Trypanis has divided his life between Greece and England; he taught at Athens University until in 1945 he became Professor of Byzantine and Modern Greek at Oxford, a post he still holds. The result is something unique in English poetry—a Greek mind working directly through the English language, so that his poetry, without ever sounding like a translation, is unlike anything that could be produced by an English poet. Furthermore, Trypanis is a classical scholar and therefore much preoccupied with ancient Greece, which has also been a magnet to English poets down the centuries; but his is a modern Greek's preoccupation, not a matter of scholarship or literary illustration but something he breathes with the air.

Why did I choose that Man (p. 142) illustrates this very clearly, since the main theme of the poem is philosophical or psychological—the changing of the personality with time—yet it is 'the Achaeans' (the name by which the Greeks are usually called by Homer) who will weep for the dead youth and build him a funeral pyre in Homeric style; and all this is not literary ornament, but a natural way of seeing things. Some of the same considerations hold true of the hauntingly tender meditation on the Nativity picture in the village church (p. 167).

RICHARD WILBUR, b. 1921 (U.S.A.)

Born in New Jersey, Richard Wilbur was educated at Harvard. served in Europe during the Second World War and now makes his living as a professor of English literature. There is no more accomplished craftsman among the younger American poets, yet his technique is never indulged in for its own sake but always adjusted very exactly to the subject-matter.

Advice to a Prophet (p. 158) deals with the problem of bringing home to the unimaginative mass of mankind just what will happen to us all if the nuclear rockets begin to fly. The world is commonly said to be 'terrified' at the prospect of full-scale war, but (the poet contends) disasters on such a scale are so hard to imagine that the mind tends to slide round them, leaving most people not terrified *enough*.

WILLIAM CARLOS WILLIAMS, 1883–1963 (U.S.A.)

A physician, William Carlos Williams has lived very nearly all his life in Rutherford, New Jersey, where his twofold vocation as doctor and poet enabled him to put down very deep roots. He was especially interested in the problem of creating a speci- fically American idiom in poetry—see his volume of essays, IN THE AMERICAN GRAIN, 1925—and among other efforts in this direction he wrote a vast epic poem, *Paterson*, which takes the New Jersey town of that name and traces the development of its character from Indian times to the present.

Williams is a poet of very positive attitudes, a celebrant of the joys of everyday living; I have included his tiny poem *This is just to say* (p. 118) as a token example of this. *Tract* (p. 161) shows

Williams in his Whitmanesque mood—exhorting, even bully-
ing, and at the same time with an all-embracing charity and
constructiveness.

W. B. YEATS, 1865–1939

No one, as far as I know, would question the statement that
Yeats is the greatest poet the English-speaking peoples have had
for a hundred years. His Irish nationality, which kept him about
equally removed from both the English and American literary
traditions, has meant that his influence has straddled both
countries; since his death there has probably been no considerable poet anywhere in the English-speaking world who has not
owed something to him. I say 'since his death' because a poet
like T. S. Eliot, who began writing at a time when Yeats had not
yet come into his full power, forged his poetic armoury without
reference to Yeats; but this was out of the question for anyone
who began after Yeats had published THE TOWER (1928) and
THE WINDING STAIR (1933).

Eleven of Yeats's poems are included here; it would be impossible to annotate them without writing an essay on his
work, but a few remarks are in order. The two earliest poems
here, *To a Friend whose work has come to nothing* (p. 172) and
Easter 1916 (p. 145), are both products of Yeats's involvement in
Irish political and social affairs. The 'friend' was Lady Augusta
Gregory, Yeats's devoted supporter, and his ally in the struggle
for an Irish theatre which would reflect the national consciousness. What precise scheme of hers had 'come to nothing' on this
occasion matters less to the student of Yeats's poetry than the
attitude he recommends, an indomitable stoic pride and a pur-
suit of the 'difficult' for its own sake. *Easter 1916* celebrates the
Easter Rebellion of that year which inaugurated the period of
violence leading up to the formation of the Irish Free State in
1922. Though a nationalist (he later became a Senator), Yeats

was not in the confidence of the extreme revolutionaries, and the Easter rising took him by surprise; at first he was indignant with the rebels for throwing away their lives, but within a few months their deaths had come to seem to him heroic. In the second section of the poem, 'that woman' is Maud Gonne, with whom Yeats was in love for years but whom, for various reasons, he never married. A fiery nationalist, she had involved Yeats in much political activity, of which his opinion can be seen in these four lines. Rejecting Yeats, she married a man named MacBride, the 'drunken, vainglorious lout' whom he nevertheless now finds the generosity to honour, along with the rest, as a hero. The man who 'kept a school' was Patrick Pearse, and 'his helper and friend' the poet Thomas MacDonagh. They are mentioned, along with James Connolly, an old companion of Yeats and Maud Gonne, in the roll-call of names at the end. The poem captures, among other things, the sense of wonder one feels at times of heroic action, that people one has known in everyday life, at 'counter or desk', and never thought of as anything but ordinary, suddenly reveal themselves as heroic; not only wars and revolutions, but shipwrecks, train crashes, mining disasters, can suddenly reveal the 'terrible beauty' of heroism—and thus the poem both celebrates and transcends its immediate subject. It is instructive to compare *Easter 1916* with run-of-the-mill poems about heroism such as *The Charge of the Light Brigade* or *Drake's Drum*, or—more seriously—with the other poems on the same theme in this book. *An Irish Airman Foresees his Death* (p. 141) finds Yeats still treading the border-line between public and private life; the airman, Major Robert Gregory, is important to the poet because he died heroically, because he was Irish and because he was Augusta Gregory's son. Robert Gregory's character, and the nature of that 'lonely impulse of delight', are described more fully in the long poem *In Memory of Major Robert Gregory*, written at the same period.

The Collar-bone of a Hare (p. 116) is from the same volume as *An Irish Airman Foresees his Death* and shows how far public themes were from capturing all his attention, even at this time. The hare, a lonely, untamable animal, is a recurrent symbol for Yeats—see the beautiful short lyric *Memory*.

A Prayer for my Daughter (p. 87) comes very close to stating the philosophy by which, as a mature man, Yeats lived, especially in its last three stanzas. *Lullaby* (p. 105), *After Long Silence* (p. 108) and *Mad as the Mist and Snow* (p. 64) are numbers 16, 17 and 18 in a sequence which Yeats called, perhaps to indicate their essentially lyrical nature and as an invitation to composers to set them, *Words for Music Perhaps*.

A Prayer for Old Age (p. 175), no less than *The Collar-bone of a Hare*, expresses the contempt Yeats was always apt to feel for the safe, the tame, the institutional—a contempt which he reconciled easily enough with his love of 'custom and ceremony'.

Long-legged Fly (p. 42) deals with a recurrent Yeatsian theme, that of power and greatness. Each stanza takes one human being who achieved legendary stature—Caesar the great emperor, Helen of Troy, whose face 'launched a thousand ships, And burnt the topless towers of Ilium', and Michelangelo, the mighty artist. These people are not raucous or restless; their minds move on silence as naturally and unpredictably (and as miraculously) as a water-skater gliding on the surface of a stream.

Finally, *Lapis Lazuli* (p. 57) embodies one of Yeats's most central and cherished beliefs—that life, however tragic, must be lived with a certain flair and style, and that the value of great art is that it leads us into a region where even tragedy and heartbreak are acted out in a high fashion and not submissively endured; 'Hamlet and Lear are gay', not in the obvious sense that they laugh and make jokes, but in the same way as the ancient Chinamen carved from lapis lazuli are gay; they have tragic resilience. This is bound up with Yeats's doctrine of The Mask, which is too complex to be summarized here, but which any full consideration will take into account.

Topics

POETRY AND THE THEATRE

One hears, constantly, of a 'revival' of Poetic Drama. Just as, in every period, the history books describe the middle classes as 'rising', so the literary surveys describe the poetic drama as for ever being revived. When was it most fully alive? In the age of Shakespeare, obviously, for that age would have been a wonderful age of dramatic verse even if our greatest poet had not been a man of the theatre. And for some time after Shakespeare verse continued to be used in the theatre without any sense of strain or unnaturalness. When the English drama revived after the Puritan ban on the theatres, and a new generation of playwrights, headed by Dryden, began a new age, it never occurred to them that verse was obsolete. True, they had a serious problem: given that no art can start unguided from nothing, what models were best to follow? Should they go back to Shakespeare? They did not doubt his greatness, but he was at the wrong distance from them in time; after half a century the greatest writer seems old fashioned; later on, he becomes safely 'historical'. Should they seek the fountain-head and take their models from Greek and Latin drama? Or should they learn from the new classical theatre that had been so triumphant across the Channel? The third solution triumphed in practice, however good the arguments may have been on all three sides; you may read the whole debate, set out in the form of an evening's conversation between three London gentlemen, in Dryden's *Essay of Dramatic Poesy*, and it is clear that Dryden could see the attractions of all three answers, as he could see the virtues both of rhyming and blank verse on the stage. But, finally, it was Racine and Corneille who were taken as masters.

and when Shakespeare's plays were re-staged in the Restoration period they were always adapted in various ways to make them conform to a taste basically French.

Increasingly, after the Restoration, verse tended to be used in high-flown and dignified plays; Restoration comedy was realistic, and realism (as Ben Jonson had shown) talks down-to-earth prose on the stage. This identification—poetry for tragedy and loftiness, prose for comedy and shrewdness—is important because it left the verse drama unprotected against the wind of realism that was soon to blow through the theatre. Theatre-goers, as well as actors and managers, came to associate verse with special occasions, prose with the kind of plays that dealt with their own lives and problems. After the success of Lillo's realistic play *The London Merchant, or George Barnwell*, in 1731, realism and prose were more firmly in the saddle, and gradually the lofty, tragic play lost ground to the comic. We remember Sheridan and Goldsmith from the eighteenth-century theatre, as we remember Lillo, but we have (as theatre-goers) forgotten Johnson and Addison.

In the nineteenth century the poetic play became firmly associated with the study rather than the stage. Virtually all the major nineteenth-century poets wrote verse plays, and yet their combined genius did not produce one significant page of theatrical history. Wordsworth, Coleridge, Byron, Shelley, Keats, Beddoes, Tennyson, Browning, Swinburne, all put some of their most formidable energies into writing plays, and none of them has lived as a dramatist. The decline of the verse drama was already almost complete, but the prestige of some of the Victorian poets, and of the famous actor-managers who liked to speak verse that sounded vaguely Shakespearean, kept a certain amount of it before the public for most of the nineteenth century, and it was not until the impact of Ibsen and his disciple Shaw, who finally swept the stage clear of everything except their own brand of socially minded realism, that verse came to be regarded as definitely alien to the stage.

Poets, nevertheless, have always loved the stage, and even without a theatre to work in they have continued to write in dramatic form. Yeats, with the help of his friend Lady Gregory, undertook the colossal task of starting afresh and building a new tradition of poetic drama; he wanted to get completely clear of realism, and was drawn to the Oriental drama in which the performers wore masks, as of course they did also in ancient Greece. Yeats's dramatic work has always been controversial. His *Purgatory* is the finest dramatic poem of the century, but is it a play? (Be careful—the answer may be yes.)

Modern poets, when they turned to the theatre, learnt one lesson from the Victorian failure, and that was to keep out of the way of Shakespeare. Any play in Shakespearean blank verse is bound to challenge comparison with Shakespeare, which, since no one has ever written with his mastery, is the kiss of death from the start. Mr Eliot began with the jerky, jazz-based rhythms of *Sweeney Agonistes*, and moved on, with *The Family Reunion* and subsequent plays, to a kind of verse based on a loose twelve-syllable pattern, which can achieve the effects of poetry without intruding itself as 'verse' to an audience trained on prose. This is a highly individual solution, and he can be seen groping towards it in his early essay, *A Dialogue on Dramatic Poetry*, which makes an interesting comparison with Dryden's *Essay*. Other poets have tried other ways. W. H. Auden, in collaboration with the prose-writer Christopher Isherwood, gave us two plays in the 1930's, *The Dog Beneath The Skin* and *The Ascent of F6*, which used a hotch-potch method, very effective, of contrasting scraps of prose and verse, swift changes of mood and tempo and a general air of brilliant improvisation.

Louis MacNeice, Stephen Spender, Lawrence Durrell, Anne Ridler and a number of other poets have faced the problems of verse drama from their own standpoint. But none of them has had much success with hard-bitten theatre audiences and harder-bitten managements. The theatre in our time has been a prose theatre in the wake of Ibsen, Shaw and Wilde. Only for a few years after about 1950 was there any box-office money in verse plays; those were the years when Mr Eliot's *The Cocktail Party* and *The Confidential Clerk* were drawing big houses in London and New York, and when Mr Christopher Fry, using a verse based on Eliot's but a language thinner and more feathery, caught the public imagination with half a dozen verse plays, notably *The Lady's Not for Burning* and *The Dark is Light Enough*. But even during these years it was the solid prose fare of Rattigan, Priestley and Graham Greene, plus the more intellectual version of the same thing offered by Arthur Miller and Tennessee Williams, that drew the real business.

At the moment the Eliot-and-Fry vogue has died down, though their plays are by no means forgotten; theatre managements have gone back to their settled conviction that to stage a verse play is to walk straight into the bankruptcy court, and we are left wondering where the next break-through will be attempted. There are those, and in some moods I am among them, who think that the real 'poetic drama' of our time is to be found in writers who do not use verse at all; Samuel Becket, for instance, or (with more reservations) Ionesco and his followers in the 'theatre of the absurd'.

On the other hand we may feel, if we care for poetry, that the tradition of thousands of years is not so easily set aside. The tragic masterpieces of the ancient Greek theatre, the Renaissance drama in every country in Europe, even the occasional untypical masterpiece like Ibsen's *Peer Gynt*, are there to remind us that verse has reigned over the stage at some of its greatest moments and can reign again. Drama is a form of ritual; even the most realistic modern play begins by assuming a great many conventions. In Greece it was linked closely to religious festivals, and when after centuries of darkness the stage was once again lit up in medieval Europe, its first beginnings took the form of a development of Christian ritual. There are certain moments in every church service which resemble drama, and the first dramatists of the post-classical world took as their starting-

226

point those portions of ritual in which the priest and his servers acted out some symbolic fragment of the Christian faith. This development has been summed up concisely by Mr Peter Arnott in his *Introduction to the Greek Theatre* (Macmillan, 1959).

It [i.e. English medieval drama] had its origins in religious celebrations, this time in the Mass. As a form of worship this is itself highly dramatic, and the Bible stories embodied in it at particular festivals—the Easter story of the Resurrection, or Christ's birth in the stable at Christmas—lend themselves readily to dramatic treatment. Drama began in England, so far as we know, with the Resurrection story. Some priest had an inspiration: the story could be brought home to the people more vividly if instead of being read by one voice, the words of the angel guarding the tomb and of those searching for Christ's body could be given to different speakers. This done, there were at once the rudiments of a play. A similar treatment was applied to other stories. As time went on, the conception was extended. The speakers began to move about the church, using different areas for different parts of the story as they seemed appropriate. The altar could symbolize Christ's tomb, or the manger, and form a focal point for the simple action. Eventually the plays were taken out of the church altogether into the streets. The whole Bible story from the Creation to the Redemption and beyond was dramatized in short episodes, each played by one group of citizens. Comic and topical elements were added. At first purely traditional, the plays came to be written down and evolved into the great local cycles that we still possess today. So from the simple inspiration of one priest who wished to bring the Gospel home to his flock came the drama and a considerable body of dramatic literature.

Today we are very remote from that world. But are we as remote as we think? The world-wide success of the German

227

dramatist Bertolt Brecht, who believed passionately in the popular spirit as a guide to all art (a belief that led him to spend his last years working under the Communist régime in Eastern Germany), argues the contrary. Brecht was a poet, if not a particularly good one, and sprinkled his plays liberally with snatches of song. The recent revival of folksong in every form, the eager appetite for anything from traditional Irish dirges to the repertoire of a singer like Josh White, probably indicates an unslaked thirst for a rough, popular verse that expresses the longings and moods of everyday life. Will some of this find its way on to the stage? Or will the next attempt be made as the last few have been, by scholarly, critically minded poets like Eliot?

One thing is beyond dispute: poets have very little affinity with novelists—the number of good novels written by poets is very small—but a great deal with dramatists. The poet, when he leaves the confines of his lyric art, goes not in the direction of prose fiction but straight towards the nearest stage. He wants to hear his words spoken; it is significant that a number of modern poets (notably Dylan Thomas, Henry Reed and Louis MacNeice) have written admirable plays for radio. W. H. Auden has done notable work in the field of opera; Mr Eliot has given more than ten years uninterruptedly to the theatre; in America Archibald Macleish and others have drawn large audiences to see plays in verse.

The whole question of verse drama, clearly, is still wide open. It is sometimes cynically said that a verse play can succeed as well as a prose play, provided it is five times as good. But will this always be the case?

And if we are to have a verse theatre, who is to act in it? The modern actor is accustomed to, and has been trained on, a prose repertoire. Can we expect him to adapt? If not, where are our verse-actors to come from? From the Shakespearean theatre? Or, as Yeats believed, from a new school of acting in which the traditions of the realistic theatre will be abandoned?

Modern life is to some extent shaped by 'Mass media of communication'—all those things which enable a large number of people to be reached quickly with information, entertainment or persuasion. The first 'mass medium' was the popular newspaper, which grew up in the 1870's; at that time the Power of the Press, as it was solemnly called, seemed unshakeable, but in our day the newspaper has become less influential than radio and television, while as a means of entertainment its thunder was stolen by the cinema before 1918. Mass media cost an enormous amount of money to operate, and therefore deal mostly in material that has a wide popular appeal; hence they easily become identified with vulgarity and slickness. There is, however, no essential reason why a film, or a radio or television programme, need be more vulgar and commonplace than a book. The English language, after all, is a mass medium, invented by the English people as a means of communication. Our concern here is with the effect, if any, of these media on poetry.

Printing, which was the first mechanization of a hand industry, had a profound effect on life in every civilized country. Up to the sixteenth century, oral disputation was the commonest means of spreading knowledge; scholars would travel from university to university with a thesis they were prepared to defend against all comers, and the audiences which gathered to listen to the debate would acquire their learning by ear. The printing press killed this, and also killed rhetoric as an important subject of study. Other changes followed. Printers insisted on standardization of spelling, and this led in turn to a speeding-up on the part of the reader. Finally things reached the state in which we find them today, when the average person reads very rapidly and silently, grasping the words in clusters and hearing nothing inside his head.

Private, solitary reading, which takes in words through the eye at a fast rate, is obviously very well suited for many kinds of material. Newspaper articles, for example, and the more primitive kinds of fiction, are written to be gulped in this fashion: taken slowly, they become intolerable. But the more meat there is in what we read, the less effective we find this silent skimming. In a novel, for instance, we read fast and silently during long stretches, but at crucial moments—or during important dialogue or memorable description—we slow down to something approaching the speed of the speaking voice. Nobody tells us to do this; we do it because if we are enjoying the story, and imaginatively entering the author's world, we need to savour what he is giving us.

Poetry, however, makes a sterner demand. It insists on being read entirely at this slower pace. To read a poem at the same speed as a newspaper article is simply an impossibility. The words in a poem are not hieroglyphics, intended to convey a meaning to the eye and thence straight into the mind, like traffic signs. They are words in the full sense—sounds, originally coined to apply to objects or notions, and making a substantial part of their impact *through* sound.

For this reason poetry has not been very well served by the printing press. It has tended to be pushed aside in favour of the novel, which grew up during the printing-press era and is ideally suited to it. The habits fostered by a civilization based on print are largely hostile to poetry. In particular, the universal practice of silent reading, of seeing the words but not hearing them, is fatal to the poet. His words must make their impact through sound and rhythm as well as through their dictionary meanings. Indeed, the reason why young children put up no such barrier against poetry as one often finds in adults is because the child enjoys a poem as a kind of song, even as a kind of dance. Professor C. S. Lewis has some wise remarks to make here:

At some schools children are taught to write out poetry they have learned for repetition not according to the lines but in 'speech-groups'. The purpose is to cure them of what is called 'sing-song'. This seems a very short-sighted policy. If these children are going to be lovers of poetry when they grow up, sing-song will cure itself in due time, and if they are not it doesn't matter. In childhood sing-song is not a defect. It is simply the first form of rhythmical sensibility; crude itself, but a good symptom not a bad one. This metronomic regularity, this sway of the whole body to the metre simply as metre, is the basis which makes possible all later variations and subtleties. For there are no variations except for those who know a norm, and no subleties for those who have not grasped the obvious. (*An Experiment in Criticism,* Cambridge University Press, 1961)

If many school-teachers make it their business to stamp out the first signs of 'rhythmical sensibility', the children they teach will probably have been robbed for ever of the chance to appreciate poetry. For nothing they will find in the world of the printed book, newspaper and magazine can possibly do anything to restore their sense of verse as a series of attractivesounds. And if they read poetry as if it were prose, they will naturally find that straight prose does the job better—and turn away from the poets altogether.

At least, that was the case a generation ago. But this is where we circle back to the topic of mass media. For radio (wholly), film and television (partly), are aural media. They work through the ear. Under their influence, humanity is once again entering a culture based on the spoken, rather than the written word.

Naturally the written word will always be important, and the book, as the cheapest and most convenient means of distributing and storing the written word, will never lose its central position. But already it has ceased to be an absolute dictator. A civilization based entirely on the eye has given place to one based, at least partly, on the ear. In this world the poet has a better chance against the novelist. The enormous number of long-playing records made in recent years by poets, and by actors and others reading the great poetry of the past, testifies that the chance is already being seized. Many of the poets in this book, for example, have issued records; in some cases, notably that of Mr Eliot, they have recorded virtually their entire output.

The usefulness of this, to the reader with a particular interest in the work of a poet, is immediately obvious. To have not only the book but the record on one's shelves, to be able to listen, as often as one feels inclined, to the poet's own rendering of his work, helps to bridge the gap between poet and reader. Often a difficult passage will become clear at once when the poet's own intonation shows how he means it to be taken. Or a poem that has seemed dull will spring into arresting and memorable life when one associates it with the individual voice of its author. (I myself was converted to Robert Frost's poetry by hearing it read by the poet.)

Yet some puzzling questions remain. Is the poet's reading of his own work inevitably the only 'right' one? Is there, indeed, one 'right' way to speak a poem, and are all the other ways merely a delusion and a hindrance? Compare, for instance, Mr Robert Speaight's reading of the *Four Quartets* with Mr Eliot's own; both are superb; is one the 'right' one because it is the poet's, or is the other 'right' because it comes from an actor with a long experience of using his voice professionally? Do voice-training, and all those skills that used to be described as 'elocution', come into the matter at all?

These questions apply primarily to the long-playing record, which (it might be argued) is not yet a mass medium. But what about the other media? Do you listen to poetry broadcasts on the radio? If so, which interests you more: to hear a poem you are familiar with, and which you can enjoy in a new rendering without having to keep your attention at full stretch to follow the 'meaning', or to be introduced to poems new to you?

Now to cinema and television. Do you think poetry can be helped, or merely hindered, by the accompaniment of images? (Many poets have been interviewed on television, and asked to say something about their work, but this is not the same thing.) Several well-known poets have shown themselves to be excellent film directors; one of them, Jean Cocteau, has called the cinema 'a dream that can be dreamt by many people at the same time'—a remark that may help to explain why it is that poets have so often been interested in the cinema. Certainly a poem like *The Waste Land*, which was written when the cinema was still new and exciting, uses many of the techniques of the film—rapid changes of focus, tracking, panning, fragmentary dialogue and in general a use of the kind of sharply visualized detail that we see in our dreams. For dreams, of course, are not 'dreamy'; they are vivid and precise.

There are undoubtedly other cases in which a poet seems to have been influenced by a medium of communication. And the question is whether the recent revival of interest in the theatre, and the less spectacular but undoubted recovery of a public for poetry, are associated with the change from a print-culture to a culture in which words are spoken aloud.

Index of Poets

Index of First Lines